CONSUMER GUIDE
TO A FLATTER
STOMACH

CHARLES T. KUNTZLEMAN AND THE
EDITORS OF CONSUMER GUIDE ®

PUBLISHED BY POCKET BOOKS NEW YORK

Contents

Making yourself look and feel better can become a habit.
No matter what your sex and age, you can take the
CONSUMER GUIDE® program one step further by
exercising with weights.

However hectic your schedule, you can still exercise to
reduce and firm your waist. We show you exercises you can
do in the privacy of your office, in spare moments behind
your desk, during your lunch hour, and even some you can
do whether you're brushing your teeth or in a crowded
room.

There are some simple precautions you can take to avoid the
aches and pains that come from overexertion.

Exercise can significantly increase the ease and reduce the
risks of pregnancy and birth. Often, you can continue to
exercise through much of your pregnancy. Then there are
exercises that will ease you back into your regular exercise
program. There are also exercises that can reduce menstrual
discomfort.

There is some good exercise equipment available. There is
also some that is worthless and even some that is dangerous.
We also look at some of today's popular weight-loss
theories and programs. Some are fraudulent, and some are
suspect.

Exercises to ease you into and out of your regular exercise
sessions and help you avoid sore muscles.

Exercises that you can substitute for others in the
CONSUMER GUIDE® program.

A chart of the number of calories expended during some
common activities.

Manufactured in the United States of America
1 2 3 4 5 6 7 8 9 10

POCKET BOOKS, a Simon & Schuster division of
GULF & WESTERN CORPORATION
1230 Avenue of the Americas, New York, N.Y. 10020

Library of Congress Catalog Card Number: 79-87546
ISBN: 0-671-82728-6

Illustrations by Mike Muir

Forward

A flat, sexy stomach. You want one—everyone does. You want the trim, narrow waist of a movie star or the flat, hard gut of an athlete. And why not? A good-looking belly makes you look and feel good. Improving the appearance of your belly usually means that your posture will improve and that nagging aches in your lower back will "magically" vanish.

Think of the inconvenience, not to mention the physical discomfort, that a flabby, protruding tummy causes you. Clothing must be selected with care. If you are a man, your three-piece suit must have a full cut, and the buttons must be moved or the back must be let out. You must keep the last button on your vest open, although only you know that you're not doing it for stylish purposes.

If you're a woman, you find your pants fitting everywhere except in the waist. So you drift over to the rack displaying big overblouses, even though the tailored look is in. But the real test comes in the summer. Do revealing summer fashions reveal what you'd like them to reveal? Or must you forego the current trend in favor of a wardrobe of muumuus and similar drapery?

Of course, you can suck in your belly. But after a few minutes or a few hundred yards, the exaggerated posture becomes uncomfortable. Before long, you decide "the heck with it" and let everything hang out. You've given up.

But this need not be the case. No matter how far you have let yourself go, you can make a comeback. You can flatten your stomach. You can regain the shape you thought was lost forever. Before reading on and deciding whether you need this book and program, ask yourself a few questions: Do you slouch? Does your back hurt? Can you feel your stomach muscles with your hands, or are they buried beneath layers of fat? Are you disgusted with the constant pressure at your waist from pants that are always too tight? At the first possible moment, do you discard those clothes for something more comfortable, something with an elastic waistband? How long does it take for that red mark around your waist, caused by pinching pants, to disappear?

Think back, now. How often do you use age as an excuse for your expanding waistline? If you don't use age as an excuse, have you ever joked about your weight, particularly if it seems to settle in one certain area? Are you like the person who says, "I can just see my stomach growing," as she bites into her third sugar donut? Finally, is your waist larger than when you were 18 (women) or 21 (men)?

6

If you answered yes to any of these or if any one of these describes you, then you need the CONSUMER GUIDE® Flatten Your Stomach program. You really can't afford to pass up this book—unless you want to live the rest of your life using one excuse after another.

We will show you how to flatten your stomach in four easy steps—steps that will make you healthier, more self-confident, attractive, and comfortable. The consultants and staff of CONSUMER GUIDE® have polled and worked with experts in the field of exercise physiology and fitness to develop a program that will work regardless of your body type, current physical condition, age, or sex. It's a program that emphasizes aerobic exercise, special tummy flattening exercises, and exercises that can be done almost anywhere at any time.

This is a program that you must do for yourself. No one can do it for you. It is your responsibility if you want to trim your waistline, flatten your stomach, and improve your overall well-being. We will give you the information and guidelines, but you must put this information into action.

Today is the best day to begin this program. Forget about tomorrow; just pretend for now that it doesn't exist. "Tomorrow" is the magic word in a procrastinator's vocabulary. It's a comforting word, but also a dangerous one. On one hand, it symbolizes all our good intentions; it's always there for us to make our fresh start. But on the other hand, tomorrow never comes; there's always another one and another one after that. "Tomorrow" is every exercise program that we really did intend to start but that somehow never got off the ground.

The CONSUMER GUIDE® Flatten Your

Stomach program will take only a few minutes of each day, but it will give you a reward that will last a lifetime. The program will introduce you to a whole new world—one of thinking, doing, and looking your best. You will lose something you have been carrying for, perhaps, years—a bulging stomach. But once you are rid of it, you will never be happier. Chic clothes, a smart, young-looking appearance, and a general feeling of health and confidence will be yours.

But remember: To win this important battle, you must think "today," not "tomorrow."

The Health Benefits of a Sexy Stomach

In this automated age, few of us maintain our bodies as they ought to be maintained. It used to be that people's normal daily activities were enough to keep their bodies firm and trim. But today, we ride rather than walk; we play games on an electronic screen rather than on a playing field; and we use every labor-saving gadget imaginable. There are even electric vegetable peelers to make our dinner preparation easier.

Our lives today simply don't require enough steady physical exertion to keep our bodies fit and healthy. And what happens to our bodies when we do not exercise them? Those nearly perfect youthful bodies begin to develop fat places, skinny places, sags, and bulges. Although we stop growing in height, we often continue to grow in the middle, especially when we have sit-down jobs. A flabby potbelly is the result of a life without enough exercise. And the result of that potbelly can be poor health. Back pain, varicose veins, a greater risk of hernias, poor elimination, greater risk in surgery, an increased tendency to overeat, and mental depression are all possible rewards of a bay window and sagging waistline.

Let's take a closer look at some of the specific health problems often associated with carrying too much fat around the stomach.

Back Pain

Dr. Hans Kraus, a back specialist whose thousands of patients have included presidents, movie stars, and athletes, feels that back pain often is due to a lack of exercise. In addition, the doctor says most back surgeries are not necessary; in fact, he says therapeutic exercises are effective alternatives to surgery in 80% of all back pain cases. Dr. Kraus feels that most pain in the lower back is muscular in origin, and that the most likely culprits are the muscles of the stomach area. According to Dr. Kraus, the prevention and treatment of disabling back disorders are so simple that they are sometimes overlooked. Studies have demonstrated that in most cases, the abdominal muscles of persons with chronic back conditions are less than one-third as strong as their back muscles. Such muscle imbalance can be the cause of a person's back problem. But the real sources of the problem, Dr. Kraus points out, are inactivity and tension.

Seventy million Americans will have some type of back pain during their lifetimes. The newsletter "New York Executive Health Examiner" reports that at least 25 percent of the sedentary, middle-aged executives it polled had some form of back trouble. The problem is that the business of making a living while sitting down makes us particularly susceptible to low back pain. A lack of physical activity causes our abdominal muscles to weaken and sag.

A sagging waistline throws the body posture out of kilter. The added weight causes the pelvis to drop in front and raise up in the back. This tipping can occur because the abdominal muscles are too weak to hold the pelvis in place. Due to this misalignment of the pelvis, the part of the spinal column that is attached to the pelvis rotates forward; then, the lumbar region (small of the back) tips forward and causes a "swayback" condition. The sway causes the vertebrae of the spine to squeeze together, which in turn puts pressure on the nerves in the area. The result is low back pain. Many times that pain can be traced to the position that people with bay windows take to keep their balance. They increase the curve of the lower back by throwing their shoulders back and their stomach and hips forward.

The muscle structure of the abdomen is so designed that the muscles crisscross to hold the organs in their proper places. Over the years, however, the soft life takes its toll and weakens these marvelous muscles. As a result, the internal organs push against the abdominal wall. Finding little or no resistance, the organs literally push the abdominal wall outward, causing the middle-age bulge.

A flat tummy—one that has strong muscles and minimal fat—reduces your chances of back pain. Abdominal muscles that are adequately exercised will hold your abdominal organs in place. They also will keep your pelvis in proper alignment. And

11

if you have no excess weight around your middle, your pelvis won't tend to tip in the first place.

Varicose Veins

Varicose veins can be caused by weakened tummy muscles. When your stomach muscles are weak, they are unable to hold your abdominal organs— stomach, intestines, liver, pancreas, etc.—in place. These organs then push against the abdominal wall and slip downward, where they put pressure on the large veins that return blood from your legs. The pressure is like a dam on the blood that's coming back up toward your heart. As a result, the veins don't function properly and the blood in them pools and pushes the veins toward the body surface, ultimately causing the unsightly condition we call varicose veins. Keeping your abdominal muscles firm reduces the chances of your abdominal organs slipping and putting pressure on your veins, and thereby lessens the likelihood of varicose veins developing.

Poor Elimination

If weak muscles let your abdominal organs slip out of their proper places, the weight of the organs can cause abnormal bends and twists in your large and small intestines. The slippage may also remove some normal bends and twists. This phenomenon increases your chances of constipation. Closely allied to this is the possibility that when your abdominal muscles are weak, they have less of a massaging effect on your small and large intestines. That is, they are less likely to help push food along toward elimination.

Hernias

A hernia, or rupture, happens when an organ, such as your stomach, pushes out between the muscles of your abdominal wall. Although a hernia may occur in other parts of your body, it happens most frequently in the abdominal area. The basic cause of a hernia is a sudden or prolonged increase of pressure from within the abdominal cavity. Severe sneezing or coughing, or lifting an extremely heavy object can create the pressure that will precipitate a hernia. Properly conditioned abdominal muscles can reduce the likelihood of an abdominal hernia. Firm muscles help hold the internal organs in place during stress and are less likely than weak muscles to separate as the pressure on them increases.

Surgical Risks

When a surgeon operates, he starts with the assumption that the patient will have a perfect abdomen, one that is just like the ones pictured in a medical textbook. But all too often, that isn't what the surgeon finds upon opening the patient's abdomen. If the patient has allowed his abdominal muscles to get flabby, his organs may have slipped out of their "textbook" locations. The surgeon must then either enlarge the incision or manually search for the proper organ. In either case, the risk of severe shock to the patient greatly increases.

For years, surgeons have been reporting that they prefer to operate on people who have a minimum of body fat. There's good reason for that preference. If the surgeon must cut through a large amount of fat in order to get to the real problem, the procedure is naturally going to take more time than if he were able to go directly through a wall of lean muscle. And as operating time increases, so does the danger to the patient. Not only that, but fat tissue is simply messy to cut through, and more effort is required to keep the incision clear.

All of this doesn't mean that you will die in surgery if you have weak stomach muscles and a lot of body fat. But remember this: the death rate during surgery of overweight patients is much higher than that of patients of normal weight. You may never need surgery during your lifetime. But if you do ever need it, you'll have a much easier time, both during the surgery and while recovering from it, if your body is lean and firm.

Muscles and Appetite

There is some speculation that people who have firm abdominal muscles may have more control over their appetites than people who have flabby muscles. As you eat, your stomach expands. When it presses against your abdominal muscles, you start to feel full. This feeling of fullness will occur sooner if your muscles are firm than it will if they are saggy. If your muscles are not firm, your stomach can expand considerably before it pushes against them. Of course, this feeling of fullness is only a temporary experience, but it may keep you from eating too much at one time. And although this may or may not have implications with respect to weight control, it has implications with respect to the fat circulating in your blood stream. It has been shown that people who eat large amounts of food at one meal tend to have higher levels of cholesterol and triglycerides, both of which can be factors in developing heart disease.

Mental Health

We touched on this earlier. When your stomach looks good, you feel good about your overall appearance. And feeling good about yourself has a direct bearing on your mental health. It's just that simple. A flat, sexy stomach not only helps you physically, it helps you mentally as well.

Body toning is one of the most noticeable benefits of an exercise program. Tone is appearance—that condition in which the muscles are naturally well-shaped and visually appealing. Your abdomen will firm up and, instead of an ugly protrusion of flab, there will be a flat, solid wall of muscle. And the benefits will extend beyond appearance. Your health and sense of well-being will improve.

A body with tone is a body in harmony with itself. It can do what it is supposed to do—like a well-tuned violin or the finely-tuned engine of a racing car.

Your
Natural Girdle

To most people, the word "girdle" implies discomfort. It brings to mind visions of daily battle, of tugging and twisting an absurdly tiny garment up past flabby thighs, over a broad "back porch," and around a protruding stomach.

But did you know that nature has provided you with a girdle that is more effective and comfortable than anything that any girdle manufacturer can promise you? Nature's girdle will control your waistline, will provide complete freedom of movement, and will never ride up or down. It can relieve you of lower back pain, will give you the support you need to carry yourself gracefully, and it will adjust automatically to the muscular stresses of pregnancy and childbirth. Mother Nature has equipped you with a true "24-hour girdle" that is so comfortable that you "won't believe it's a girdle."

But there's one catch. To keep your natural girdle in good working order, you must take proper care of it. You must exercise it daily.

By now, you've probably guessed that your natural girdle is the muscles of your abdomen. Unfortunately, most Americans let these muscles become weak and saggy from disuse. They turn then to synthetic girdles to supplement their weak muscles, to hold in their tummies, and to improve their posture.

A Belly By Any Other Name

People use many different words to describe their stomach areas: tummy, belly, and middle are some of them. Since these are the terms that people use most often, they are the ones that we have used throughout this book. Before going any farther, we should define what we mean when we use these terms so that you will know what parts of the body we are talking about at any given time.

Abdomen (belly): the area of your body located just below your navel. If you have too much fat, this is the part of your body that sags down in front.

Waist: the area of your body located between your rib cage and your hips on the sides of your body.

Tummy: the area of your body around your navel. After you've eaten a full meal, this is the area that may feel distended.

Midriff: the area of your body crossing just below the rib cage and near the diaphragm.

Abdominal region (middle, stomach): the region of your body that extends from the bottom of your breastbone to your pubic area in front, and from your ribs to your hips on your sides. Although the stomach is actually a digestive organ and can't, in itself, be fat, it's common to hear someone say, "He has a fat stomach."

How Your Natural Girdle Works

Consider for a moment how your body is constructed. First, there are the bones of your skeletal system. They are the framework of your body, providing support and protection. Attached to this bony framework are muscles that give your body its basic shape and its power to move. In and around some of your muscles are deposits of fat that insulate and cushion the muscles and the other organs beneath the muscles. These fat deposits may vary in thickness from a fraction of an inch to several inches, depending on their locations, your genetic makeup and, of course, how many calories you've been taking in.

The structure of your stomach region is no different than that of any other part of your body. Above, below, and in back of your stomach are the bones that make the outer border for your stomach. Above are the ribs and the breastbone. Below are the hip (pelvic) bones. In back are the bones of the spinal column. Muscles are attached to the bones in various places. These muscles crisscross your stomach region and form your abdominal girdle. Throughout these muscles, as well as in front of and behind them, are fat cells that act as storage tanks for body fat.

The muscles of your abdominal girdle work in harmony to perform many functions. They give shape to your waist, support the organs of your abdominal cavity, squeeze the contents of your stomach and intestines during digestion, protect your internal organs from blows, and keep your pelvis in its proper position. Although these muscles play only a small part in your turning and bending movements when you are standing up, they play a very large role in such movements when you are lying on your back. That's because when you are standing up, your weight is centered over a small area. But, when you are lying down, your weight is spread over your whole length, and your abdominal muscles must be called upon to overcome this weight.

Your abdominal girdle also plays an important part in your appearance. For your abdomen to appear well-proportioned, your waist should be a few inches smaller than your shoulders, chest, and hips. But for your waist to be that way, your abdominal muscles must be strong enough to stay firmly in place and to hold your organs in.

The Muscles of Your Abdomen

There are four groups of muscles that make up your abdominal girdle. Each group is actually a pair of muscles—one on, or starting on, the right side of your abdomen and one on, or starting on, the left.

The *rectus abdominis* muscles run vertically from the middle of your rib cage to your pubic bone. When these muscles are properly conditioned, they give the front of your abdomen a rippled, or "washboard," appearance. A washboard belly is often considered attractive in men.

The external and internal oblique muscles run on an angle from your ribs to your hips. They are also attached to a broad fibrous sheath of tissue that lies beneath the *rectus abdominis*. The obliques

The Muscles Of The Abdomen

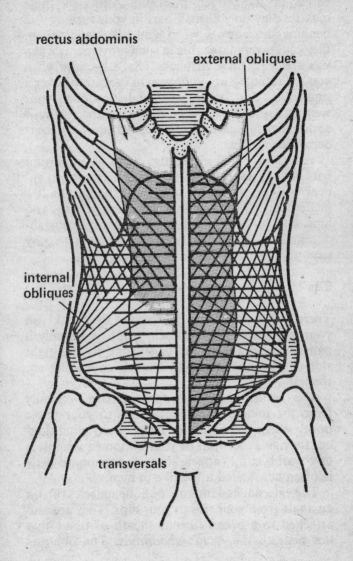

rectus abdominis

external obliques

internal obliques

transversals

help hold the organs of your abdomen in place and aid you in making twisting movements with your body.

The transverse muscles run horizontally. They start behind the *rectus abdominis* muscles and go to the hips, backbone, and ribs. The main function of the transverse muscles is to help hold the contents of the abdominal cavity in place.

All those muscles form the crosshatch of your natural girdle. As we mentioned earlier, on top of, behind, and throughout the fibers of the muscles are deposits of fat that provide cushioning and insulation for the muscles and the organs beneath them.

There are two other muscles that are also very important, and which must be considered when discussing the abdominal area. They are the *psoas* major muscle and the *iliacus* muscle. These two muscles work so closely together that they often are thought of as a single muscle and are called, together, the *iliopsoas* muscle. The *psoas* is attached to the spinal column and the thigh bone, and the *iliacus* is attached to the hip and thigh bones. These muscles act together to flex the thigh. They also aid in rotating the thigh outward.

When you bend over with your thigh bone locked in place, as when you touch your toes without bending your knees, the *iliopsoas* muscle aids in flexing the trunk toward the thigh. Similarly, when you sit up from a prone position, but don't bend your legs as you do so, the *iliopsoas* is the muscle that brings you up. The other four abdominal muscles are not the prime movers when you do straight-leg sit-ups. Those four muscle groups may help, but the *iliopsoas* is the most important. Due to this phenomenon of anatomy, straight-leg sit-

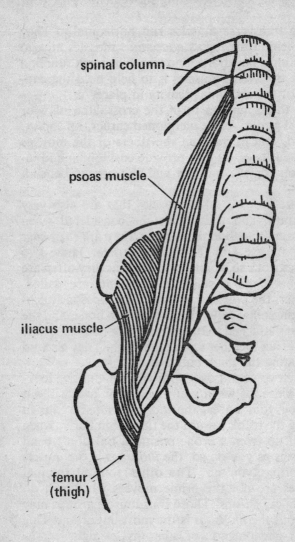

spinal column

psoas muscle

iliacus muscle

femur
(thigh)

ups are not good exercises for flattening your stomach. They affect a muscle that has almost no bearing on your appearance. Besides that, the *iliopsoas* is normally exercised when you walk, run, and climb stairs. Consequently, it does not need additional exercises.

To really exercise your abdominal muscles, the *iliopsoas* muscle must be immobilized. To do that, you must bend your knees when you do sit-ups. When sit-ups are done with the knees bent, the other abdominal muscles come into play and are exercised vigorously.

The difference between the action of the *iliopsoas* muscle and the action of the abdominal muscles is an important concept when it comes to flattening your stomach. Later, when you begin the CONSUMER GUIDE® Flatten Your Stomach program, you will understand the importance of doing all the sitting up exercises with your knees bent.

What is
Your Problem?

Most people are unaware that an unattractive stomach may be the result of a variety of factors, and that it's usually caused by a combination of these factors. In order to get rid of your belly, you have to start with what causes it. The three principal factors in the development of an unsightly stomach are slack abdominal muscles, obesity, and heredity.

Don't confuse obesity with overweight. *Overweight* means you weigh more than a standard height-weight chart indicates that you should for a person of your height. Such a chart might indicate, for example, that a 25-year-old woman who is five feet tall should weigh about 110 pounds. But the chart is based on average heights and weights; no distinction is made as to the proportions of bone, muscle, organ, and fat tissue, all of which vary from person to person. *Obesity,* on the other hand, means an excessive amount of body fat.

An overweight man or woman actually may be well within the normal range of "fatness" or even comparatively lean. A professional football player is a good example. A halfback may be six feet tall and weigh 215 pounds. According to the height-weight chart, 215 pounds is too heavy. How can this be?

The football player exercises a lot and is heavily muscled. Much of his weight is muscle tissue; only 10 percent of his body weight is fat (about 15 percent is the ideal proportion for men). So, he looks good despite being "overweight." Many athletes, both male and female, are overweight but not obese.

On the other hand, a person can be obese without being overweight according to the chart. It is possible to weigh just what the chart says you ought to weigh, but still have a total percentage of body fat that is several points over what is desirable and healthy.

Many American males fall into this category. A typical case might be the athlete who weighs 170 pounds in his senior year of college. He graduates and eventually becomes a sedentary member of the desk set. Because he exercises less now than when he was in college, the muscle tissue in his body has become correspondingly less dense, and therefore, less heavy. At the same time, he has added a little fat to his body. All else being equal, he should lose weight in order to keep his proportion of fat to muscle constant. Although the former athlete still weighs 170 pounds, his muscle-to-fat ratio has changed in favor of the fat. He has become obese, although he is not actually overweight.

That is what seems to have happened to President Ford, who claimed during his early presidency that he weighed about the same as he did when he played football at the University of Michigan. He failed to point out, however, that his waist measurement increased from 32 inches (when he was at the University of Michigan) to 38 inches by the time he assumed the presidency.

So far, we've seen how you can be overweight without being obese and how you can be obese without being overweight. You can also be both obese and overweight at the same time.

A study of adult males, conducted by Dr. Ancel Keyes, an eminent Minnesota physiologist, indicates that there is a direct relationship between obesity and the amount of exercise a person normally gets. Dr. Keyes found that the men in his study who were in ideal physical shape—those who were overweight but carried very little body fat—regularly engaged in physical labor. However, the men who were overweight, and also obese, led very sedentary lives.

Testing Yourself

There are three quick tests you can perform on yourself to determine what kind of shape your stomach is in, although you probably won't need to take all three to find out. You'll know pretty quickly whether you are pleased with yourself. If you aren't pleased with what these tests tell you, go on and take the Pinch Test and the Poke Test discussed below. They will tell you specifically whether your problem is too much fat, weak abdominal muscles, or both.

The Mirror Test. The quickest, easiest way to find out if your stomach is too fat is to get undressed and stand in front of a full-length mirror. Be critical. Do you like what you see in your abdominal region? Have your body contours changed since you were younger, since you changed jobs, since last fall, etc.? If your stomach sags where you don't want it to sag, or if your waist protrudes, you are probably moving into the obese range—if you're not already there.

The Weight/Waist Gain Test. Recall what you weighed when you were 21 if you are a man or 18 if you are a woman. If memory fails, you can dig out old medical records. You can assume that each pound gained and each one-half inch of waistline gained since that time represents an accumulation of fat and weakened stomach muscles.

Chest/Waist Measurement. Stand with your shoulders pulled back and your chest expanded to its fullest. Measure the circumference of your chest just beneath your armpits. Be certain that your tape measure is flat and level. Then, with your stomach in a relaxed position (not sucked in or forced out) measure your waist at the navel. For men, the chest should be five inches greater in circumference than the waist. For women, the difference should be ten inches. If it's not, it's an indication that your stomach is too fat.

Pinch Test

Take this test to determine whether your unattractive middle is due to excess fat accumulation. Using only your thumb and forefinger, try to grasp the skin and fat anywhere on your waist, midriff, or abdomen. If you can pinch more than three-quarters of an inch (man) or one inch (woman), your problem is due to too much body fat. This pinch test is based on a technique in which physiologists use an instrument called a skinfold caliper to measure body fat. The National Center of Health Statistics in Washington points out that "skinfolds permit a closer estimate of body fat than do the tables of relative weight . . . Skinfolds are becoming established as the easiest and most direct measure of body fat available in the doctor's office, the clinic, or—on a large scale—population survey." Since most of us are not able to take a skinfold caliper test, the pinch test is a reasonable alternative.

If you find that you exceed the three-fourths or one inch criteria established by CONSUMER GUIDE® fitness experts, your condition is the result of not burning off enough calories to compete with the number of calories that you eat. To reduce your fat, you must engage in aerobic exercise four times a week. This is a type of exercise that gets your whole body moving. It gets your heart beating faster and your lungs breathing deeper. Some good aerobic exercises are walking, jogging, swimming, cross-country skiing, and bicycling. These activities burn calories and fat from your body. It doesn't matter where the fat is, whether it's on your stomach, belly, waist, or midriff. When you engage in aerobic exercise, it comes off all over your body, not just from one site.

The Poke Test

The second significant reason for a sagging stomach is weak abdominal muscles. Muscles can become so flabby from disuse that it is difficult to determine whether what you see is muscle tissue or fat tissue. For many adults, the reason for a sagging, unattractive stomach in an otherwise well-built body is weak stomach muscles. Take a good look at a healthy youngster who is not obese. You can see the definition of his or her abdominal muscles. Now look at your own stomach. Is it flat? Does it have a washboard look? Probably not.

Healthy children are constantly on the move. That accounts for their natural ability to maintain flat abdomens without trying. Add to this the fact that the weight of a child's internal organs is much less than that of an adult's. A child's abdominal muscles don't have to work nearly as hard as an adult's to keep his organs in place.

Of course, as adults mature, their muscles grow in size and strength. But the average adult fails to subject his abdominals to the kind of physical stresses they should have in order to remain in condition. So, by the time a person reaches his or her middle or late 20s, these muscles are no longer functioning as nature intended them to. They no longer hold the intestines and stomach in place with springy elasticity. Instead, the abdomen begins to resemble a burlap sack packed full of sausage. The muscles get weaker. The internal organs slip even more and press against the abdominal wall, and the cycle becomes more and more vicious. The organs press more, the muscles get weaker, the organs slip even more, and so on.

The situation is complicated by the fact that your posture is also affected. Weakened abdominal muscles allow the pelvis to drop in front and rise in the back, thereby exaggerating the bay window condition and creating a swayback condition. Soon the intravertebral discs of the spine become squeezed. The result is low back pain.

But how do you know if the muscles of your body are too weak? Here's where the poke test comes in. Tighten your stomach muscles. Using your index finger, poke it into the muscles of your midriff, stomach, abdomen, or waist. If your finger gets lost or buried in the stomach and doesn't feel much resistance, your muscles are too weak. You need to begin a calisthenics program for the midsection of your body. If you still aren't sure after the poke test, try to do a sit-up with your knees bent. If you can't do more than one sit-up, you have weak muscles in the midsection of your body.

Exercises such as the stomach-whittling calisthenics described in the next chapter are the only effective way to deal with potbellies caused by weakened muscles. These exercises strengthen the *rectus abdominis,* oblique, and transverse muscles. Conditioning these muscles will make them strong enough to hold your organs in place and keep your pelvis in line, which in turn will give you an attractive appearance. Waist belts and girdles won't help these muscles. Such devices are not only uncomfortable, but they lead to further muscular degeneration by doing all the work for the muscles. If used constantly, these devices may allow the muscles to so weaken that you're even more susceptible to hernias. And, of course, when you remove the girdle or belt, your potbelly is still there.

Some people who have tried abdominal exercises report no success. No wonder. They didn't use the right exercises. Many purported stomach exercises are not effective at all. There are several muscle groups in the upper and lower abdomen. Several exercises must be performed to affect the various muscle groups. The CONSUMER GUIDE® Flatten Your Stomach program provides exercises for the various parts of your stomach.

Your Body Type

There's something else that must be considered—your body type. People come in different shapes and sizes. Big ones, small ones, fat ones, skinny ones, and many in between. Bone structure, the number of fibers in the muscles, the length of the intestines, and a host of other factors play a major role in your basic body type. And these factors are determined by heredity.

For years, scientists have tried to classify people according to their body types. There have been varying degrees of success. Recently, somatotyping has come into use. Somatotyping is a method of classifying the human body into three basic types by estimating the balance of fat, muscle, and bone. Understanding more about your body type will go a long way in helping you determine how successful the CONSUMER GUIDE® Flatten Your Stomach program will be for you.

Somatotyping divides human bodies into three types: endomorphic, mesomorphic, and ectomorphic. An endomorph possesses a roundness or softness to his body. He has little muscle development and small bones. His weight is centered in the front of the body around the abdomen. He's usually extremely poor in athletic events that require support of the body, speed, agility, endurance, or jumping. His talent in sports may be for golf, archery, or swimming. If this is your body type, it may be difficult for you to lose your pudgy middle, because you are very prone to putting on fat and have a difficult time losing it. The problem is complicated by the fact that the activities you probably enjoy are bicycling or swimming. Therefore, your range of activities is limited. You have a natural tendency for softness or roundness; consequently, your stomach may always tend to look a little more pudgy than your friends'.

We don't want you to be discouraged if you are an endomorph. But we do want you to understand your limitations. You will make progress using the CONSUMER GUIDE® program, but it may take you longer than it takes other people, and you still may not get an "ideal" stomach. Fortunately, very few people fall into this extreme category. Most people who think they are endomorphs are really finding an excuse for being in bad shape.

A mesomorph is muscular and big-boned. Noted for hardness and ruggedness, he or she normally is of moderate height and is long necked and broad shouldered; a mesomorph has a large chest, a relatively slender waist, and broad hips. Mesomorphs usually excel in activities that require strength, power, agility, and endurance, such as wrestling, football, lacrosse, and baseball. People with this type of build usually have a tendency to put on weight after giving up sports. They develop the classic "beer belly." Fortunately for these people, once they engage in aerobic kinds of exercise and also do calisthenics for their stomach area, they make rapid improvements. Fat seems to be lost quickly and the abdominal muscles also firm up very quickly. These are the lucky ones who get washboard stomachs.

An ectomorph is thin-muscled and thin-boned. His or her body looks fragile and delicate. The trunk is short. The neck, arms, and legs are long. There is very little fat on his or her body. Generally, however, an ectomorph's posture is rather poor because he or she lacks the muscular strength for proper support. Activities such as badminton, tennis, and endurance running are an ectomorph's best ventures. Usually, this person has a very low percentage of body fat. His or her particular problem often is weak abdominal muscles. Traditional calisthenics tend to produce striking results for this individual. Although this individual tends to be linear throughout his or her body, abdominal exercises will help to produce a nice washboard effect. Generally, abdominal problems tend to be below the navel and are exaggerated by poor posture. An ectomorph's appearance will improve markedly if he or she follows the CONSUMER GUIDE® program, although progress may be slow.

Of course, not all of us fall into these extreme categories. There are very few pure endomorphs, mesomorphs, or ectomorphs. We simply have a tendency towards fatness, muscularity, or thinness.

You have to decide in which category you belong. Are you more of an ectomorph, a mesomorph, or an endomorph? Once you know the classification, you'll know what kind of work is cut out for you. The following points will help you know what to expect from the CONSUMER GUIDE® Flatten Your Stomach program:

1. If there's a tendency in your family toward obesity (your mother and father tended to be fat), you can conclude that you are on the endomorphic side. If that's the case, expect your results to be less dramatic than those of a mesomorph or ectomorph.

2. If at one time you had a good physique, but lately things seem to have gone to pot, it's probably

an indication that you're a mesomorph. Lucky for you. You will see dramatic changes with the CON-SUMER GUIDE® program.

3. If there's a natural tendency toward thinness in your family, you'll find the exercises outlined in the CONSUMER GUIDE® program effective in helping to flatten your stomach. It will simply take you a little more time than it would a mesomorph.

Taking Stock Of Yourself

The best way to see your fitness needs clearly is to summarize them and record them on paper. In that way, you'll have a reminder of exactly why you are following the CONSUMER GUIDE® program. The summary will help you establish your goals and will serve as a reference point for gauging your progress.

To take stock of your present condition and to determine your needs, ask yourself all the questions listed below. Then, use your answers to set up a chart like the one you'll find following the questions.

To assess the overall condition of your stomach, answer these questions:

1. Are you displeased with the appearance of your middle when you look into a full-length mirror?　　　　　　　　　YES　NO
2. Is your chest less than five inches (man) or ten inches (woman) greater than your waistline?　　YES　NO
3. Have you gained more than five pounds and/or has your waistline increased more than

one-half inch since you were 21
(man) or 18 (woman)?   YES NO

If you answered any of those questions "yes,"
you have a problem. You are carrying too much
fat, or you've allowed your stomach muscles to
become too weak to do their job properly. To
clarify exactly what your problem is—fat, muscle
weakness, or both—answer these questions:

1. Can you pinch more than three-
   quarters inch (man) or one inch
   (woman) anywhere on your
   stomach?   YES NO
2. When you poke your index
   finger into your stomach
   muscles, do you find little
   resistance?   YES NO
3. Are you unable to do more than
   one sit-up (keeping your knees
   bent)?   YES NO

If you answered the first question "yes," your
problem is too much fat. If you answered either the
second or the third question "yes," your problem
is that your muscles are too weak.
    Finally, what is your body type? Do you tend to
be an endomorph, a mesomorph, or an ectomorph?

Endomorph: expect slow improvement.
Mesomorph: expect rapid improvement.
Ectomorph: expect average improvement.

Now you are ready to jot down what you've
learned from these questions. Make a list like the

one below and keep it handy for reference.

Date: _____

My waist size: _____

My chest size: _____

My weight: _____

My body type: _____

Results of pinch test: _____

Results of poke test: _____

Number of sit-ups: _____

What I'd like to change about what I see in the mirror (sagging belly, protruding tummy, etc.):
_____

My waist size should be: _____

My weight should be: _____

Exercises to Whittle Your Middle

On the following pages are 27 exercises that you can use to whittle your middle. These exercises will firm up flaccid stomach muscles and give them the tone they had when you were a youngster. The exercises will strengthen your abdominal muscles so that your pelvis will be held in place, thus preventing an exaggerated pot belly and the low back pain that may go with it. Finally, these exercises will help keep your abdomen flat so that your stomach, intestines, and other organs stay in their places.

CONSUMER GUIDE® fitness experts used two basic criteria in selecting these 27 exercises: safety and effectiveness. Of the hundreds of exercises considered, these 27 were selected as the best from both standpoints.

The 27 exercises are arranged in six groups. The first three groups focus on toning up the lateral muscles of your stomach (the obliques and the transverse muscles). The remaining three groups focus on the middle, or frontal, muscles of your stomach (the *rectus abdominis*). Naturally, there is cross benefit between the exercises. For maximum benefit, you should do at least one exercise from each group each time you work out.

The exercises are arranged in each group by increasing difficulty. This is done so that as you do the exercises you will know which ones to progress to as your body adjusts to a particular exercise. If you're able to do more than 30 repetitions of a particular exercise, it is too easy for you. Therefore, you should select another exercise or do the exercise in such a way that it is more difficult for you. For example, in the beginning, you may be able to do 10 regular sit-ups. But, as your stomach becomes stronger and in better condition, you will soon be able to do 30. When that happens, you should consider doing the sit-ups on an incline. Because the incline makes the exercise more demanding, you may only be able to do eight.

Although any of these exercises will help flatten your stomach by toning up weak abdominal muscles, you'll get the most benefit from them if you do them in a well-planned program that also includes exercise specifically intended for burning off excess fat. Look through the exercises in this chapter; perhaps try a few of them. Then, go on and read the next chapter, "Fat: You Must Move To Lose," which will tell you what you must do in order to reduce your body fat as you tone your muscles. After you have read both chapters, you will be ready to begin your custom-tailored CONSUMER GUIDE® Flatten Your Stomach program.

Exercises for Lateral Muscles
Group I

Single Side Leg Raises

1. Lie on your right side, your right arm extended above your head (palm against the floor), your head resting on the extended arm. Place your left hand on the floor in front of your waist for stability.
2. Raise your left leg to at least a 45-degree angle.
3. Lower your leg to the starting position.
4. Repeat several times. Then turn and do the exercise on your other side.

Exercises for Lateral Muscles
Group I

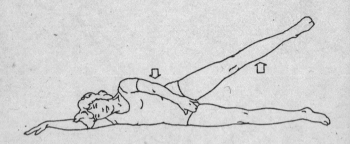

Single Arm and Leg Raises

1. Lie on your right side, your right arm extended above your head (palm against the floor), your head resting on the extended arm. Keeping your left arm straight, place it across your waist.
2. Raise your left leg to at least a 45-degree angle.
3. As you lower your leg, simultaneously raise your left arm. By the time your leg is back to starting position, your arm should be at about 45 degrees.
4. Return your arm to starting position; as you do so, raise your leg again.
5. Repeat several times. Then turn and do the exercise on your other side.

Exercises for Lateral Muscles
Group I

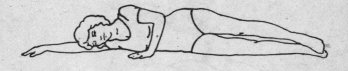

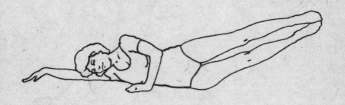

Side Double Leg Raise (6 inches)

1. Lie on your right side, your right arm extended above your head (palm against the floor), your head resting on the extended arm. (If you wish, you can bend your right arm and rest your head in your right arm.)
2. Keeping your legs together, raise them six inches off the floor.
3. Lower your legs to the starting position.
4. Repeat several times. Then turn and do the exercise on your other side.

Side Double Leg Raise (12 inches)

Same as the previous Double Leg Raise, except raise your legs 12 inches off the floor.

Exercises for Lateral Muscles
Group II

Crossovers

1. Lie on your back, legs together, arms extended at right angles to your body.
2. Raise your right leg to a vertical position.
3. Keeping your leg straight, lower it to the floor on your left side. Attempt to touch your right toe to your left hand.
4. Return your leg to vertical and then to starting position.
5. Repeat the movement with your left leg, attempting to touch your left toe to your right hand.
6. A toe-touch to the left and one to the right constitute one exercise. Repeat several times.

Exercises for Lateral Muscles
Group II

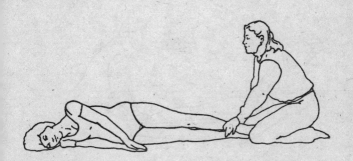

Side Curl-Ups

1. Lie on your right side, arms extended downward in front, hands about six inches in front of your hips. Have a partner hold your feet down or brace them under a piece of furniture.
2. Curl your body upward several inches.
3. Return to starting position. Repeat several times.
4. Turn and do the exercise on your left side.

Exercises for Lateral Muscles
Group II

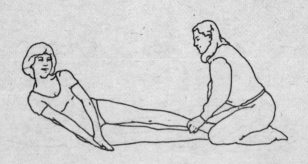

Side Sit-Ups

Same as Side Curl-Ups, except curl your body upward as far as possible.

Side Sit-Ups (Arms Extended)

Same as Side Sit-Ups, except extend your arms above your head.

Exercises for Lateral Muscles
Group III

Double Knee Lifts

1. Lie on your back, arms extended at right angles to your body, knees drawn up to your chest.
2. Keeping your knees together, touch the floor to the right of your body with your right knee.
3. Return to the starting position.
4. Touch the floor to the left of the body with the left knee and return.
5. Touching first to one side, then to the other, constitutes one exercise. Repeat several times.

Exercises for Lateral Muscles
Group III

Twist and Curl-Up

1. Lie flat on your back with your knees bent and your hands placed behind your neck or across your chest.
2. Tighten your abdominal muscles. Curl your head and shoulders up off the floor.
3. As you roll upward, twist slightly to the left.
4. Hold for three seconds.
5. Return to starting position. Repeat several times, twisting to the alternate side each time.

Exercises for Lateral Muscles
Group III

Sit-Up and Twist

1. Lie flat on your back with your knees bent and your hands placed behind your head.
2. Curl your body up into a sitting position by first drawing your chin toward your chest and then lifting your upper body off the floor. Keep your back rounded throughout the movement.
3. As you are completing the sit-up, twist your torso and touch your left elbow to your right knee.
4. Twist to the right and touch your right elbow to your left knee.
5. Return to starting position. Repeat several times. (Each time you repeat, start by touching an alternate knee.)

Exercises for Lateral Muscles
Group III

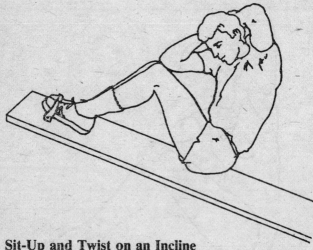

Sit-Up and Twist on an Incline
(If an incline board is not available, do Up-Oars and Twist instead)

1. Lie on your back on an incline board, knees bent and feet secured by a holding strap (or held down by a partner), hands behind your head.
2. Curl your body up to a sitting position by first drawing your chin toward your chest and then lifting your upper body off the incline. Keep your back rounded throughout the movement.
3. As you are completing the sit-up, twist your torso and touch your left elbow to your right knee.
4. Twist to the other side and touch your right elbow to your left knee.
5. Return to starting position. Repeat several times. (Each time you repeat, start by touching an alternate knee.)

Exercises for Lateral Muscles
Group III

Up-Oars and Twist
(Alternative to Sit-Up and Twist on an Incline)

1. Lie flat on your back with your legs extended, arms extended down the center of your body.
2. Raise your upper body off the floor and simultaneously bend your knees, sliding your feet toward your buttocks. Don't arch your back.
3. As you curl upward, twist your upper torso toward the right and also extend both arms to the right.
4. Return to starting position. Repeat several times, twisting to alternate sides.

Exercises for Frontal Muscles
Group IV

Head and Shoulder Curl

1. Lie on your back with your knees bent at a 90°
   angle, feet on the floor, hands and arms crossed
   on your chest. (You may, instead, place your
   hands behind your neck or place your arms
   along the sides of your body).
2. Tighten your abdominal muscles. Roll your
   head and shoulders up off the floor.
3. Hold for three to six seconds.
4. Return to starting position. Repeat several
   times.

Exercises for Frontal Muscles
Group IV

Look-Up/Curl-Down

1. Lie on your back, your lower back area touching the floor, knees bent.
2. Curl your head and upper body upward and forward to about a 45° angle. (Be sure you curl up; don't jerk and don't arch your back.)
3. Hold briefly and return to the starting position.
4. Repeat several times, then proceed with the Curl-Down/Look-Up exercise.

Exercises for Frontal Muscles
Group IV

Curl-Down/Look-Up

1. Sit on the floor with your knees bent and your hands behind your head.
2. Slowly lower your upper body downward to a 45° angle or until you feel your stomach muscles begin to pull.
3. Hold briefly, then return to starting position.
4. Repeat several times.

Exercises for Frontal Muscles
Group IV

Sit-Ups

1. Lie on your back with your knees bent and arms
   across your chest. You may also extend your
   arms along your sides or over your head, or
   place your hands behind your neck.
2. Curl your body up into a sitting position by first
   drawing your chin toward your chest and then
   lifting your upper body off the floor. Keep your
   back rounded throughout the movement.
3. Sit up as far as possible.
4. Return to starting position. Repeat several
   times.

Exercises for Frontal Muscles
Group IV

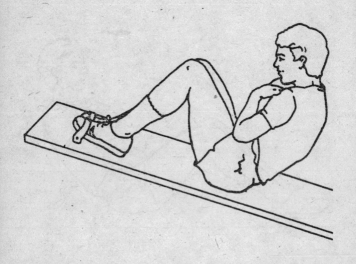

Sit-Ups on an Incline
(If an incline isn't available, do the Up-Oars instead)

1. Lie on an incline board, knees bent and feet secured by a holding strap or held by a partner. Place your arms across your chest or at your sides.
2. Curl your body up into a sitting position by first drawing your chin toward your chest and then lifting your upper body off the incline. Don't arch your back. Sit up as far as possible.
3. Return to starting position. Repeat several times.

Exercises for Frontal Muscles
Group IV

Up-Oars
(If an incline is not available for sit-ups)

1. Lie on your back with your arms at your sides, legs extended.
2. Curl your upper body off the floor and simultaneously bend your knees, sliding your feet toward your buttocks. Don't arch your back.
3. Grasp your hands around your shins.
4. Return to starting position. Repeat several times.

Exercises for Frontal Muscles
Group V

Single Leg Raise (Knee Bent)

1. Lie on your back with your left knee bent and your left foot on the floor. Extend your right leg along the floor and place your hands on your hips or at your sides.
2. Raise your right leg as high as possible, keeping the small of your back against the floor.
3. Return your right leg to the floor.
4. Repeat several times, then do the exercise with your left leg.

Exercises for Frontal Muscles
Group V

Bicycle Pumps

1. Sit with your legs extended and hands resting on the floor beside your hips.
2. Raise your legs off the floor and lean your upper body back slightly.
3. In this position, move your legs as though riding a bicycle. Be certain legs are extended while performing the exercise. Keep your back slightly rounded.
4. Each time your right leg reaches out counts as one repetition. Repeat several times.

Bicycle Pumps (No Support)

Perform the same movements as for regular Bicycle Pumps. But, as your legs start moving, lift your hands from the floor and try to keep your balance.

Exercises for Frontal Muscles
Group V

Alternate Toe Spikes

1. Lie on your back with your legs extended, arms at your sides.
2. Curl your upper body upward; as you do so, raise your left leg, and touch your right hand to your left toe.
3. Return to starting position. Curl up again, touching your left hand to your right toe, and return to starting position.
4. This completes one full movement. Repeat several times.

Exercises for Frontal Muscles
Group VI

Double Knee Raise

1. Lie on your back with your legs straight out on the floor, arms at your sides.
2. Bring both knees up as close to your chest as possible. Keep the small of your back against the floor.
3. Extend both legs upward as straight as possible.
4. Return your knees to your chest.
5. Return to starting position. Repeat several times.

Exercises for Frontal Muscles
Group VI

V-Seat

1. Sit on the floor with your legs extended and your hands on the floor next to your hips.
2. Slowly raise your legs off the floor and tilt your upper body backward slightly. Your body should form a V. (Keep your back slightly rounded.)
3. Hold for three to six seconds. (A more difficult variation is to describe a figure eight with your feet.)
4. Return to starting position. Repeat several times.

Exercises for Frontal Muscles
Group VI

V-Seat with Flutter

1. Assume the same position as for the V-Seat.
2. When in the V-Seat position, move your legs up and down in a fluttering fashion without touching the floor. Each raising of the right leg constitutes one repetition. Repeat several times.

Exercises for Frontal Muscles
Group VI

Spikes

1. Lie on your back with your legs extended, arms at your sides.
2. Curl your upper body off the floor and simultaneously raise your legs off the floor. Don't arch your back.
3. Come up far enough to touch your fingertips to your toes.
4. Return to starting position. Repeat several times.

Fat: You Must Move to Lose

Move it! To get rid of fat, you must get your whole body moving—and keep it moving.

In the previous chapter, we showed you 27 exercises for flattening your stomach by toning your abdominal muscles. But such calisthenics, in themselves, will not remove an appreciable amount of fat.

When there is too much fat in any area of your body, you have no alternative: you simply must burn more calories than you take in. The best way to burn calories is to engage in activities that keep your whole body moving. Walking, bicycling, jogging, swimming, dancing, skipping rope, cross-country skiing, and walking or running in place are some perfect examples of whole-body exercises.

Your body normally maintains a fine balance between the number of calories eaten and the number of calories burned off through physical activity. For example, if you take in 2,400 calories of food and burn off 2,400 calories as you work and play your way through the day, your body weight will remain constant. But, if you eat 2,400 calories each day and burn off only 2,300, you will have 100 calories left over. Those excess calories will then be stored as fat in the fat cells of your body until they are needed. One hundred calories don't sound like much. But if you were to do this for 35 days, it would amount to 3,500 calories. Physiologists have calculated that 3,500 calories constitute one pound of fat. If you follow this pattern of one pound every 35 days, by the end of the year you'll have gained approximately 10 pounds. And it doesn't matter what type of food you eat—calories are calories.

That is how obesity creeps up on you. It doesn't happen overnight. One year you buy a 36-inch belt, but the next year you need a 38. Suddenly you realize that you've reached a weight you never thought you'd reach—and you didn't even notice that it was happening.

People often panic when they discover this has happened to them. They immediately select a diet—usually the one that is currently in vogue. They think it's the only way to lose those extra pounds. But the dieting doesn't work. How many people do you know who have always been on a diet but always look the same? They lose weight but they gain it right back. Dr. Jean Mayer, former professor of nutrition at Harvard University, and now president of Tufts University, has said that this pattern of losing and gaining weight is the "rhythm method of girth control." Only about 8 percent of the obese are able to lose weight and keep it off.

Why can't people keep weight off once they've lost it? For one thing, dieting is not any fun. It requires truly Spartan willpower. And, judging from that 8 percent figure, most people don't have the Spartan will. But there is an even more basic reason why most people can't keep weight off.

The real problem with dieting is that it does not strike at the basic cause of obesity. And the basic cause of obesity is a lack of real physical activity. Fat accumulates not as much from overeating as from underdoing.

You probably know someone who claims to "eat like a bird" but gains weight anyway. And then there's the person who says he "eats like a horse" but never puts on weight. There's always been a tendency to disbelieve those stories, because, until very recently, the accepted "cause" of being overweight has been overeating. New research, however, suggests that both of those people may well be telling the truth about how much they eat.

Studies done at Harvard and other universities around the world have demonstrated that people who are too fat generally eat no more than the lucky ones who do not have a problem with their weight, and that most people—fat and thin—eat somewhere between 2,300 and 3,000 calories worth of food a day. The studies also have shown, however, that fat people tend to exercise far less than normal-weight people. In fact, some studies have shown that the obese spend up to four times as many hours watching TV as do thin people.

Answering The Skeptics

Skeptics like to point out that exercise isn't very effective in losing weight. They say it takes a great deal of exercise to burn off the caloric equivalent of one pound of fat. They point out, for example, that thirty-five miles of walking, seven hours of splitting wood, eleven hours of playing volleyball, or six hours of playing handball are required to burn off one pound of fat. The flaw in this reasoning is that although these equations are true, they completely ignore the *cumulative effect of exercise.* Although it indeed may take six hours of handball to burn off one pound of fat, it need not be done in a single six hour period. One-half hour of handball every day for 12 days would also burn off one pound of fat; playing handball at that rate would burn 25 to 30 pounds a year. And that's a significant amount of fat!

Some people say exercise is self-defeating because as soon as your exercise level increases so does your appetite. Not so, say researchers. The appetite of an active person does increase when he or she starts to exercise. But, when a sedentary person increases his or her activity, his or her appetite decreases. Researchers don't know yet what causes a sedentary person's appetite to decrease, while an active person's appetite increases. The cause may be physiological, psychological, or a combination of both.

There is one more important point. When people lose weight by dieting, they often remain flabby. But if you exercise while you diet or use exercise as the sole means of losing weight, your muscles will become firmer. Therefore, you will look and feel better after losing weight through exercise than you would after only dieting.

Not only can dieting leave you just as flabby as when you started, it can also leave you looking saggier. When you diet, you lose not only fat but also some bone, muscle, and organ tissue. The bone, muscle, and organ tissue are what give your body its basic shape—the shape you want to reveal by losing the fat that's concealing it. Exercise is superior to dieting as a means of losing weight because it does not result in a loss of lean body tissue. It reveals and improves, rather than removes, your natural shape.

Bill Zuti, Ph. D., and Lawrence Golding, Ph. D., set out to compare the effects of three methods of weight reduction on body weight, body composition, selected blood measurements, and physical fitness. The 25 women participating in the study were all between the ages of 25 and 40 and carried 20 to 40 pounds of excess fat. Three groups were formed: (1) eight women were placed on a diet that reduced their caloric intake by 500 calories per day, while their physical activity remained unchanged; (2) nine continued to eat as usual, but increased their physical activity to burn off 500 extra calories a day; and (3) eight reduced their caloric intake by 250 calories a day and increased their physical activity to burn off 250 calories per day. Before and after the sixteen-week period, the subjects were tested for body weight, body density, skinfold and girth measurements, and selected blood lipids (fats).

The results indicated that there was no significant difference between the groups in the amount of weight loss. The average individual weight loss in all three groups was 11.4 pounds. Thus, the study indicated that all of the methods were extremely effective in controlling weight. However, the significant finding of the study was that there was a difference between the groups with regard to body composition. Those in the exercise group and in the exercise-diet group had undergone significant decreases in body fat. The dieting group lost both body fat and muscle tissue; the exercise group lost more body fat than the dieters and no muscle tissue.

In the study by Golding and Zuti, the members of the exercise group also developed more stamina than the others; their circulatory systems were much better able to withstand the rigors of exercise. The report concluded that the use of exercise in a weight-reduction program is far superior to dieting alone in its effect on body composition and physical fitness.

Aerobic Exercise

The best activities for burning calories are those that involve your whole body. Such activities are called aerobic exercise. They are exercises that involve the large muscles of your body and are performed continuously for a significant period of time. Activities such as those we mentioned at the beginning of this chapter—swimming, bicycling, rope skipping, etc.—qualify as aerobic exercises because they are vigorous enough to engage your whole body.

During such exercise, your heart beats faster, your breathing becomes deeper, and your blood vessels expand to carry blood and oxygen to the working muscles. Your body takes in and uses a more than ordinary amount of oxygen. And using oxygen means burning calories.

When you do aerobic exercises, you use about 100 calories every 8 to 12 minutes. Aerobic activities are good calorie burners because they are continuous. There are no pauses during them.

There is a continuous flow from one movement to another. Although such calisthenics as those we showed you in the previous chapter are not, in themselves, aerobic exercises, you can make them aerobic. By doing so, you will tone your muscles and burn away fat at the same time.

How can you make calisthenic exercises aerobic? You must simply perform them in a continuous, non-stop fashion for at least 30 minutes (20 in a pinch). Continuity and duration are the crucial factors.

Unfortunately, most calisthenic routines are done in a stop-and-go fashion. So they're not aerobic. For example, you are told to do push-ups, rest, do sit-ups, rest, etc. The rest, or interruption, is the problem. For exercise to be effective in burning calories you must keep moving from one exercise to another, smoothly and without pause.

To turn what would ordinarily be just a series of calisthenics into an aerobic exercise, you might do Sit-Ups in the kitchen, V-Seats in the living room, and then, if you're getting bored with the scenery, move to the dining room for Single Side Leg Raises. The point is to move and keep moving.

Calisthenics that are steady and rhythmic, however, should not be confused with some others that may be strenuous but not continuous. A jogger, bicyclist, or swimmer is engaging in a "pay as you go" type of exercise; enough oxygen is being taken in to meet the demands of the exercise. A person running very fast or sprinting, however, is not involved in aerobic activity; the sprinter cannot possibly take in enough oxygen to keep up that pace.

Another exercise that does not permit sustained activity is weight lifting. Weight lifting may be vigorous and do wonders for the skeletal muscles of your body, but it does very little for the most important muscle—the heart. In fact, it may harm your heart. The American Heart Association Committee on Exercise points out the disadvantages of this type of sport: "Activities requiring effort against heavy resistance such as weight lifting at near maximum exertion and isometric exercises (testing one set of muscles against another or against an immovable object) do little to improve cardiovascular function and are probably not recommended since they provoke excessive, possibly dangerous (blood) pressure response." The Committee might have added that these activities don't reduce body fat, either.

The key words, then, in describing the type of exercise to be selected for removing body fat (and for heart health) are "continual," "rhythmic," and "whole-body." Exercises that consist of erratic stopping and starting are indeed exercise and may serve other purposes, but they do little to reduce your body fat or to develop aerobic endurance. The editors of CONSUMER GUIDE® magazine took this concept into account in the Flatten Your Stomach program. The result is an aerobic program that emphasizes abdominal exercises.

How Vigorously?

The benefits of aerobic exercise depend on increasing your heart rate and sustaining the increased rate for 30 minutes. The rate at which your heart ought to beat during exercise is called your "target heart rate" and is 75 percent of your heart's maximum capacity.

Your heart's maximum capacity is the number of beats it would make per minute if your body were undergoing maximum stress. A maximum heart rate would generally be 220 beats per minute, minus your age. If you are 20 years old, your maximum heart rate is 200 beats per minute. If you are 60, it is 160 beats per minute. This formula is derived from the observation that for each year you live your heart slows down by about one beat a minute.

Although 75 percent of your maximum heart rate is the ideal exercise intensity, it's more realistic to speak in terms of your target heart rate range, which is between 70 and 85 percent of your maximum heart rate. If your heart works at below 70 percent capacity, you will achieve very little fitness benefit from the exercise unless you work at it for an extended period of time or unless you were very unfit to begin with. If your heart works above 85 percent capacity, the added benefit is negligible.

Table 1 gives the maximum heart rate, the target heart rate, and the target heart rate range for ages 20 to 70 in five-year increments. You can easily calculate your own rates and range if your age falls between the increments or is beyond the chart.

When you know your target heart range, you can easily determine whether you are performing the program at the most beneficial intensity. Simply take your pulse rate at any time during the exercises. For example, you might check your pulse rate immediately after doing an Up-Oars exercise. If your heart rate is in the target area, then you are doing the exercise at a proper speed. If it is too high, you should slow down during the next series of exercises or during the walk/run in place sequence between exercises. The important principle is that you want to train, not strain.

TABLE 1. YOUR TARGET HEART RATE AND HEART RATE RANGE

Maintaining your target heart rate is the key to the CONSUMER GUIDE® Flatten Your Stomach program. Your maximum heart rate is the greatest number of beats per minute your heart is capable of. During exercise, your heart rate should be approximately 75 percent of this maximum. To obtain the fat-reduction benefits of this program, maintain a heart rate between 70 and 85 percent of your maximum for 30 minutes.

Age	Your Maximum Heart Rate (Beats per minute)	Your Target Heart Rate (75 percent of the Maximum in beats per minute)	Your Target Heart Rate Range (Between 70 percent and 85 percent of the Maximum in beats per minute)
20	200	150	140 to 170
25	195	146	137 to 166
30	190	142	133 to 162
35	185	139	130 to 157
40	180	135	126 to 153
45	175	131	123 to 149
50	170	127	119 to 145
55	165	124	116 to 140
60	160	120	112 to 136
65	155	116	109 to 132
70	150	112	105 to 128

How Long?

When trying to burn calories and fat, the longer you work out the better. At rest, your energy comes from glycogen and glucose (carbohydrates). When you sprint, you're doing anaerobic exercise (an exercise that can be done literally without oxygen). Such exercise places severe stress on your body, and you get all your energy from your carbohydrate stores. But, when you perform aerobic exercise, there's a shift in your metabolism. During the first few minutes of the exercise, about 90 percent of all your energy comes from carbohydrates and about 10 percent from fat. As you continue to exercise aerobically, the energy shift continues toward the utilization of more fat. After about 30 minutes, 50 percent of your energy comes from carbohydrates and 50 percent from fat. And when you go on for about two hours, 90 percent comes from fat and 10 percent from carbohydrates. So, you can see that it is very important that the exercise you do for reducing fat be of a long-distance variety. Remember that short bursts of intense activities burn only carbohydrates.

Aerobic exercise done over a period of weeks will improve your body's ability to consume, transport, and utilize oxygen. And, as we said earlier, using oxygen means burning calories.

To determine the minimum amount of time you ought to spend exercising aerobically each day, first estimate your caloric imbalance. A quick way to do this is to find out how many pounds you gain (or have to struggle to keep off) each year. If five pounds is your problem, you are out of caloric balance by about 50 calories per day. If ten pounds is your problem, 100 calories a day is what you are out of balance. Fifteen pounds is 150 calories. You simply add a zero to the number of pounds you struggle with each year. That will give you the approximate number of calories that you are out of balance.

For every 100 calories you are out of balance—that is, for every 10 pounds you want to lose or keep under control—you need 8 to 12 minutes of exercise per day at target heart rate levels.

How Often?

Now that you know how long and how hard, the next question is how often should you exercise each week? We recommend that you exercise a minimum of four times a week. Studies show that exercising three days a week is not enough to make fast changes in body fat. So, it becomes frustrating. Michael Pollock, Ph. D., director of the Cardiac Rehabilitation Laboratory at Mount Sinai Hospital in Milwaukee, found that exercising four days a week is more effective for body composition than two or three days. This observation was supported by some of our own recent research that showed that four-day-a-week exercise was far superior to two-day-a-week exercise in altering body composition.

You Can't Lose Part Of It

There is no such thing as spot reducing. Sit-ups may help you flatten your abdomen. But you need target heart rate exercise to burn off the fat. If spot reducing worked, people who talked a lot would have thin faces.

Drs. Grant Gwinup and R. Chelvan, and T. Steinberg at the University of California, did a study of tennis players. They evaluated players who had been playing tennis at least six hours a week for two years or more. Obviously, these people subjected their right arms to more exercise than their left. The doctors measured the circumference and the thickness of the fat at specific sites on the players' arms and took comparative measures of a control group of people who did not play the game.

As the study turned out in all cases, the circumference of the arm used to swing the racquet was larger than the less active arm. Exercise had not reduced but had increased the size of the arm. The difference in size, of course, was due to greater muscle development.

The most significant finding of the study, however, was that the tennis players as a group had less subcutaneous fat (fat stored directly beneath the skin) on both arms than did the control group. The conclusion of the researchers was that exercise, regardless of the type, reduces fat from the entire body and not merely from one specific area.

This doesn't mean that you shouldn't do traditional "spot-reducing exercises" for your broadening middle. It's just that you must understand that these exercises can only firm and strengthen the muscles. They are not likely to make you lose inches in a specific area, unless your expanding waistline is due to the fact that the abdominal viscera are pushing out against the abdominal wall.

But spot fat reducing is physiological hogwash. Research indicates that you're either born with a certain number of fat cells or the actual number is determined during the first few years of life. After that, the number of fat cells you have remains constant. When you are young and physically active, the cells stay depleted of fat. But as you grow older, and become more sedentary and burn off fewer calories than you eat, your cells act like fuel storage tanks and fill up with fat. These fat cells are located all over your body, and their location is usually determined by heredity. So, all you have to do is look at your parents, and if you find they tend to locate a lot of fat around the middle, you're probably headed in the same direction.

This fat is stored in case of an emergency, such as a period of famine, and your fat cells swell with fat for later energy use. Then, when you go into calorie deficit—that is, when you start to burn more calories than you take in—the nervous, endocrine, and circulatory systems act together to release fat for energy.

Vigorous movement of a single localized group of muscles—the stomach muscles, for instance—will not cause fat to be released only around those muscles. There are no physiological pathways for such a direct outlet. Instead, your nervous system triggers the release of small quantities of fat from the cells all over your body. The circulatory system then picks up the fat and takes it to the liver where it is converted into energy which is used by the muscles.

Summing Up

The rule of thumb is this: If you have too much fat, then you have to go into calorie deficit with a big-muscle activity that permits you to exercise at your target heart range level—Aerobic exercise. If, however, your abdominal muscles are weak, then Sit-Ups, V-Seats, and the other exercises described in the previous chapter will be effective in helping you flatten that particular area of your body. In all probability, you will require a combination of the two, calisthenics and Aerobic exercise. Many times, when people have excessive fat around their abdomens, they also have weak abdominal muscles. So, if you engage in target heart rate exercise, you should also be doing specific exercises to firm up problem areas and vice versa.

Consumer Guide® Flatten Your Stomach Program

You are ready to begin a program that will make you look better than you have for years.

You now know the best exercises for firming and flattening your stomach muscles. You also know the importance of aerobic exercise in getting rid of fat. In this chapter, we are going to show you how to put this knowledge together into a program so unique and effective that you'll be amazed by the results. But you can't wish the results. You must follow the CONSUMER GUIDE® four-step program to get the movie-star waist or the athletic gut you want.

The underlying theme of the CONSUMER GUIDE® program is continuous exercise to keep your heart rate in the target range. To keep your heart rate in the target range, there must be no pausing between exercises. CONSUMER GUIDE® staff and fitness experts designed the

Flatten Your Stomach program in such a way as to reduce the chances that your heart rate will drop below your personal target range while you exercise. We put walking in place and running in place between each exercise. This format forces you to keep moving, which helps keep your heart rate in the target range and, therefore, helps you burn a significant number of calories.

Let us show you what we mean. Look at the chart for the Step 1 program.

The chart indicates that you are to spend five to ten minutes warming up. The warm-up is important to help prepare the muscles, ligaments, and tendons of your body for more vigorous activity. In that way, there is less likelihood of an injury occurring. (The warm-up exercises are illustrated in Appendix A at the back of this book.) After you do the warm-up exercise, you should walk for a few minutes. The warm-up walk gives your heart time to adjust for the next exercise. It is very important to give your heart this warm-up time. Studies have shown that people who do not warm-up properly have significant changes in the electrical patterns of their hearts in the first few minutes of vigorous exercise, which means they can increase their chances of a heart attack if they have heart disease. It's better to be on the safe side and spend the five to ten minutes warming up your heart for more vigorous exercise.

After this warm-up period of stretching and walking, you start with the Single Side Leg Raises exercise. Do four repetitions. Then get up and walk in place for 15 seconds. After that, progress to the Crossovers exercise. Do four repetitions. Get up at once and walk in place for 15 seconds.

Next, do four repetitions of the Double Knee

STEP 1
CONSUMER GUIDE®
Flatten Your Stomach Program
Duration: 15-28 minutes

	1	2	3	4	5	6	7
			LEVELS				
Warm-Up and Walk			5-10 minutes				
Single Side Leg Raises	4	6	8	10	12	14	16
Walk in Place			15 seconds				
Crossovers	4	6	8	10	12	14	16
Walk in Place			15 seconds				
Double Knee Lifts	4	6	8	10	12	14	16
Walk Stairs (in seconds)	30	35	40	45	50	55	60
Head and Shoulder Curl	4	6	8	10	12	14	16
Walk in Place			15 seconds				
Single Leg Raise (Knee Bent)	4	6	8	10	12	14	16
Walk in Place			15 seconds				
Double Knee Raise	4	6	8	10	12	14	16
Walk (include cool-down exercises)			5-10 minutes				

Lifts. That exercise is followed by stair walking for 30 seconds. If stairs are not available, step up and down on a bench or stack of newspapers about eight inches high. The stair-walking exercise is followed by four repetitions of the Head and Shoulder Curl. The curl is then followed by walking in place for 15 seconds. The exercise after the walk in place is four repetitions of the Single Leg

STEP 1
CONSUMER GUIDE®
Flatten Your Stomach Program
Duration: 15-28 minutes

	8	9	10	11	12	13	14
			LEVELS				
Warm-Up and Walk			5-10 minutes				
Single Side Leg Raises	18	20	22	24	26	28	30
Walk in Place			20 seconds				
Crossovers	18	20	22	24	26	28	30
Walk in Place			20 seconds				
Double Knee Lifts	18	20	22	24	26	28	30
Walk Stairs (in seconds)	65	70	75	80	85	90	95
Head and Shoulder Curl	18	20	22	24	26	28	30
Walk in Place			20 seconds				
Single Leg Raise (Knee Bent)	18	20	22	24	26	28	30
Walk in Place			20 seconds				
Double Knee Raise	18	20	22	24	26	28	30
Walk (include cool-down exercises)				5-10 minutes			

Raise (Knee Bent). Next, the 15-second walk in place is performed. This is then followed by four repetitions of the Double Knee Raise. After the Double Knee Raise, walk for five to ten minutes. Gradually slow your pace during the last few minutes of the walk and incorporate the cool-down exercises found in Appendix A.

The cool-down is very important. It allows your

CONSUMER GUIDE®
Flatten Your Stomach Program
Duration: 25-30 minutes

				LEVELS			
	1	2	3	4	5	6	7
Warm-Up and Walk				8 minutes			
Jog				1-2 minutes			
Single Arm and Leg Raises	4	6	8	10	12	14	16
Jog in Place				15 seconds			
Side Curl-Ups	4	6	8	10	12	14	16
Jog in Place				15 seconds			
Twist and Curl-Up	4	6	8	10	12	14	16
Walk Stairs (in seconds)	100	105	110	115	120	125	130
Look-Up/Curl-Down	4	6	8	10	12	14	16
Jog in Place				15 seconds			
Bicycle Pumps	4	6	8	10	12	14	16
Jog in Place				15 seconds			
V-Seat	4	6	8	10	12	14	16
Jog				1-2 minutes			
Walk (include cool-down exercises)					8 minutes		

body to return to more normal levels and prevents feelings of lightheadedness after exercising.

During the first day on the program, begin at Step 1, Level 1. If during this session you find that Level 1 is relatively easy, then the next day or the

STEP 2
CONSUMER GUIDE®
Flatten Your Stomach Program
Duration: 25-30 minutes

				LEVELS			
	8	9	10	11	12	13	14
Warm-Up and Walk				8 minutes			
Jog				1-2 minutes			
Single Arm and Leg Raises	18	20	22	24	26	28	30
Jog in Place				20 seconds			
Side Curl-Ups	18	20	22	24	26	28	30
Jog in Place				20 seconds			
Twist and Curl-Up	18	20	22	24	26	28	30
Walk Stairs (in seconds)	135	140	145	150	155	160	165
Look-Up/Curl-Down	18	20	22	24	26	28	30
Jog in Place				20 seconds			
Bicycle Pumps	18	20	22	24	26	28	30
Jog in Place				20 seconds			
V-Seat	18	20	22	24	26	28	30
Jog				1-2 minutes			
Walk (include cool-down exercises)					8 minutes		

next time you exercise you can then progress to Level 2. The number of days you spend at each level is contingent upon two important factors:

1. How do you feel? If the exercises seem challeng-

STEP 3
CONSUMER GUIDE®
Flatten Your Stomach Program
Duration: 27-32 minutes

	1	2	3	4	5	6	7
				LEVELS			
Warm-Up and Walk			7 minutes				
Jog			2-3 minutes				
Side Double Leg Raise (6 inches)	4	6	8	10	12	14	16
Jog in Place			20 seconds				
Side Sit-Ups	4	6	8	10	12	14	16
Jog in Place			20 seconds				
Sit-Up and Twist	4	6	8	10	12	14	16
Walk Stairs (in seconds)	170	175	180	185	190	195	200
Sit-Ups	4	6	8	10	12	14	16
Jog in Place			20 seconds				
Bicycle Pumps	4	6	8	10	12	14	16
Jog in Place			20 seconds				
V-Seat with Flutter	4	6	8	10	12	14	16
Jog			2-3 minutes				
Walk (include cool-down exercises)					7 minutes		

ing, stay at this level until they become easier.
When that occurs, then you're ready to move to
the next level in this particular step.

2. Are you at the target heart rate level? If you are
at the target heart rate level as you are doing the

STEP 3
CONSUMER GUIDE®
Flatten Your Stomach Program
Duration: 27-32 minutes

	8	9	10	11	12	13	14
			LEVELS				
Warm-Up and Walk			7 minutes				
Jog			2-3 minutes				
Side Double Leg Raise (6 inches)	18	20	22	24	26	28	30
Jog in Place			25 seconds				
Side Sit-Ups	18	20	22	24	26	28	30
Jog in Place			25 seconds				
Sit-Up and Twist	18	20	22	24	26	28	30
Walk Stairs (in seconds)	205	210	215	220	225	230	240
Sit-Ups	18	20	22	24	26	28	30
Jog in Place			25 seconds				
Bicycle Pumps	18	20	22	24	26	28	30
Jog in Place			25 seconds				
V-Seat with Flutter	18	20	22	24	26	28	30
Jog			2-3 minutes				
Walk (include cool-down exercises)					7 minutes		

exercise program, then this level is challenging. If you find that your heart rate doesn't get up to the target zone, then you must walk in place at a faster rate or perhaps even run in place.

(In the beginning, however, you should simp-

STEP 4
CONSUMER GUIDE®
Flatten Your Stomach Program
Duration: 27-35 minutes

				LEVELS			
	1	2	3	4	5	6	7
Warm-Up and Walk				6 minutes			
Jog				3-4 minutes			
Side Double Leg Raise	4	6	8	10	12	14	16
Jog in Place				30 seconds			
Side Sit-Ups	4	6	8	10	12	14	16
Jog in Place				30 seconds			
Sit-Up and Twist on an Incline or Up-Oars and Twist	4	6	8	10	12	14	16
Walk Stairs (in seconds)	245	250	255	260	265	270	275
Sit-Ups on an Incline or Up-Oars	4	6	8	10	12	14	16
Jog in Place				30 seconds			
Alternate Toe Spikes	4	6	8	10	12	14	16
Jog in Place				30 seconds			
Spikes	4	6	8	10	12	14	16
Jog				3-4 minutes			
Walk (include cool-down exercises)					6 minutes		

ly walk in place faster and raise your knees higher.) If you're still below your heart rate target range, you should move to the next level.

CONSUMER GUIDE®
Flatten Your Stomach Program
Duration: 27-35 minutes

	LEVELS						
	8	9	10	11	12	13	14
Warm-Up and Walk			6 minutes				
Jog			3-4 minutes				
Side Double Leg Raise	18	20	22	24	26	28	30
Jog in Place			30 seconds				
Side Sit-Ups	18	20	22	24	26	28	30
Jog in Place			30 seconds				
Sit-Up and Twist on an Incline or Up-Oars and Twist	18	20	22	24	26	28	30
Walk Stairs (in seconds)	280	285	290	295	300	300	300
Sit-Ups on an Incline or Up-Oars	18	20	22	24	26	28	30
Jog in Place			30 seconds				
Alternate Toe Spikes	18	20	22	24	26	28	30
Jog in Place			30 seconds				
Spikes	18	20	22	24	26	28	30
Jog			3-4 minutes				
Walk (include cool-down exercises)						6 minutes	

If your pulse rate is above your target heart rate range, you should slow your walking pace. If that does not work, you may have to do the exercises at a slower pace. Or you may even have to work at a lower level. For the great majority of people, however, target heart rate levels will not occur at Step 1, Level 1.

Your own body is your best guide for telling you when to move from level to level. When you get to Level 14 in the Step 1 program, you're ready to move onto Level 1 of Step 2. Here you follow the same procedures, moving up through the various levels depending upon your personal feelings and your target heart rate level. This pattern is followed through Steps 3 and 4.

Notice that when you move from Level 14 of one step to Level 1 of the next step, the number of repetitions drops significantly. That's because the exercises are more and more demanding as you move up through the four steps. Also note that from Step 1 to Step 2 you progress from walking in place to jogging in place. And the number of seconds climbing stairs increases significantly.

Generally, Step 1 is a beginner's stage. When you start moving up into Steps 2, 3, and 4, you'll find them much more challenging. Step 1 is extremely important for conditioning your body to the rigors of target heart rate exercise and muscle-conditioning exercises.

Questions You May Have

Can another exercise be substituted for walking in place?

Absolutely. You can try kicking your legs to the side, which we call the fitness lope; or, you can do stride-hops, toe hops, or jump rope. (Alternatives to walking in place are illustrated in Appendix B at the back of this book.) You can do any movement that will keep your legs moving so you'll be in the target heart rate area. You might even try walking or jogging from one part of the house to another. That is, do your Single Side Leg Raises in the living room, your Crossovers in the kitchen, and your Double Knee Lifts in the den.

How can I keep it interesting?

The answer is simple. Do it to disco music. Pick some music that keeps good 4/4 time and holds a beat of about 128 to 144 beats per minute. That should do it. You'll find that the music will keep your whole body moving the entire time. If you don't like disco music, try something patriotic, like "Anchor s Aweigh" or "The Marines Hymn," or try an appropriate show tune or movie theme.

What happens if one of the exercises is too hard and the rest are rather easy?

Stay at the lower level on the difficult exercise, but progress upward as you normally would on the other exercises. It is possible to be at Level 14 on most of the exercises but only at Level 3 on another. Keep moving upward steadily. Eventually, the difficult exercise will follow. In a few instances, there may be an exercise that never catches up. But generally you'll get the hang of the exercise and you'll move upward.

How fast should I do the exercises?

That depends on your target heart rate. If you find that while you're doing the exercises your heart rate is in the target heart rate zone, everything is fine. But if you find that you're exceeding it, you then may have to do the exercises slower or not walk or run in place as fast. If you find that your target heart rate is below what it is supposed to be, then run or walk in place faster. In a few instances, you may have to do the repetitions a lot faster.

When should I take my pulse rate?
Any time. But a good time is right around the bench stepping or stair climbing. That's in the middle of the workout.

Must I do the stair climbing (or bench stepping)?
Yes. It serves as an excellent activity to burn a significant number of calories.

Must I do the running or walking in place (or one of the alternates)?
Yes, if you want to lose abdominal fat. These are the activities that burn the calories and thereby help keep your percentage of body fat low. Only in rare instances can a person afford to pass up running in place. You might be one of the very rare individuals who simply has weak abdominal muscles and very little abdominal fat. If that's the case, simply do the calisthenics. But if you're like most people, your percentage of body fat starts to increase as you get older, so you must do the walking and running in place to help keep your level of fat low.

What happens when I get to Step 4, Level 14?
That's the subject of the next chapter, "Make Your Stomach Stronger."

Make Your Stomach Stronger

What happens when you complete the final level of the last step of the CONSUMER GUIDE® Flatten Your Stomach program? You go one step further. You continue to do the Level 14 exercises of Step 4, but you do them with weights.

Don't let the word "weights" scare you away. We are speaking of weight training, which must not be confused with power lifting. Power lifting is a sport and involves lifting extremely heavy weights. Power lifting is what we recommended *against* when discussing aerobic exercises earlier. Proper weight training involves lifting weights that are no heavier than you are comfortable with.

Actually, moving from one step to the next in the CONSUMER GUIDE® Flatten Your Stomach program is, in itself, a form of weight training. The weight you are lifting is your own body. When you move to the next step in the program, the exercises are more demanding. That is, your body is positioned so as to increase the resistance your muscles must overcome in order to lift it. So, when you reach the last level of the program, the next logical step is to increase the weight of your body, thereby increasing the resistance your muscles must overcome.

You don't have to add much weight to your body when you move into the weight-training stage of the Flatten Your Stomach program—between one and five pounds will do. A weighted vest and weighted shoes or boots are the most convenient kinds of weights to use. Such equipment, designed specifically for weight training, is available in many large sporting goods stores and from catalogue merchandisers. But, if you can come up with a homemade alternative, that's fine; just about anything can be used for weights—books, canned goods, etc.

As for jogging in place and climbing stairs, continue to follow the guidelines for Level 14 of Step 4—that is, 30 seconds of jogging and 5 minutes (300 seconds) of climbing. However, as you feel your body adapting to the demands of the jogging and climbing, simply step up the pace. Do them faster or raise your legs higher. This will help keep your heart rate in the target range, and you'll continue to burn a significant number of calories.

Misconceptions About Weight Training

There are many misconceptions about weight training. Let's clear up some of the most common ones.

Will weight training make you muscle-bound?
A muscle-bound person is one who has enlarged

his or her muscles to such an extent that they have become inelastic. Occasionally, some weight lifters who do not follow proper training techniques become what appears to be muscle-bound. But you needn't fear that. Using weights will simply help you firm up and strengthen your muscles without any adverse effect on their elasticity or your agility and general body flexibility.

Will weight training make a woman masculine?

Women will not develop masculine-type muscles or a masculine shape. That's because of their endocrine make-up. Women will maintain and even enhance their natural female shape through weight training. Many beauty contest winners and contestants are trained with weights.

Will muscles turn to fat as soon as you stop active training?

Muscles are muscles and fat is fat. One will not change into the other. You can, however, reduce the volume of fat and increase the volume of muscle in your body if you make minimal efforts to keep yourself in relatively good physical shape.

Does weight training have age restrictions?

Many elderly people work out regularly with weights. And some of the most dramatic results can be achieved by people of middle age.

Does weight training involve lifting extremely heavy weights?

Absolutely not. We've already mentioned this. You use only the amount of weight with which you are comfortable. The point is that, as you continue a program of weight training, you become comfortable with progressively increasing amounts of weight. You never lift more than feels right to you.

The Principles of Training

There are eight important principles that underlie the process of physical training. You must understand these principles in order to use weight training effectively.

Adaptation. If your muscles are made to work harder, they will eventually adapt to the increased stress. For example, suppose you are now able to do 30 sit-ups. When you first attacked this exercise, you found ten to be quite demanding, maybe even exhausting. But after several weeks, you were able to do 30. What happened was that your body adapted to the exercise load. Once your body has adapted, however, your abdominal muscles will not become appreciably stronger if you continue at that level. But, by adding a small amount of weight to your body, you will increase the stress on your muscles. And again, your muscles will gradually adapt to the new load.

Overloading. Once your stomach muscles have adapted to an exercise, they must be made to work harder. This is called overloading. Increasing the number of repetitions of the exercise is one way to overload your muscles. But weight training is more efficient.

If you are able to do 30 sit-ups, for example, it is time to overload your muscles. You can do this by placing a weight, such as a book, on your chest. Having thus overloaded your front abdominal muscles, you may be able to do only 10 to 15 repetitions. Over the next few weeks, however, you'll gradually be able to increase the number of repetitions until you get to 30. Your body will have adapted again to the exercise load. So, it's time to overload once more.

It's important that you don't add too much weight when you overload. If you do, you won't be able to do the exercise properly, and you will experience too much fatigue. From one to five pounds will do for most people. This gradual process of overloading, adaptation, then overloading again is called progression.

Progression. If you add too much weight on your body at one time, your body will rebel. You will either not be able to do the exercise, or you will become so tired while doing it that any benefits will be cancelled out. Therefore, you must add weight progressively. For example, instead of adding ten pounds to your chest when doing sit-ups, you might just add one, one and one-half, or two pounds. Your body will be the best guide as to how much weight you can comfortably handle. When your muscles adapt to this weight, you can add another small amount of weight. In this way, you will gradually, but safely, reach a ten-pound overload.

Specificity. Specificity refers to the fact that improvements made in training are directly related to the type of training followed. For example, conditioning your abdominal muscles will strengthen them. But it does not increase your aerobic endurance and, therefore, will not significantly help you keep your weight down. Similarly, an endurance type of program, such as running, will do little to improve the strength of your abdominal area. Also, exercises that strengthen the frontal muscles of your abdomen won't effectively strengthen lateral muscles, and vice versa (although there is nearly always some cross benefit). In order to strengthen your entire abdominal area, you must do exercises (whether with or without weights) both for the frontal muscles and the lateral muscles. To also keep your weight under control, you must do the exercise aerobically as well.

Retrogression. When doing exercise, you may find that on certain days your performance seems to be off the usual pace. Try as you might, you may not be able to do 30 sit-ups on the incline with a one-pound weight, even though you have done this for the past three weeks. The reason for this fall-off in performance—called retrogression—is not known. But it probably has something to do with the ability of your body to mobilize its resources for meeting the overload imposed upon it. When the body adjusts, you then begin to reach your typical level of performance.

Occasionally, retrogression is a result of a poor diet, inadequate sleep or rest, lack of motivation, or improper conditioning. Regardless of the cause, it's important that you constantly monitor your current condition. Be sure that your nutritional intake is adequate, that your rest and sleep are sufficient, and that your training techniques are proper. If the retrogression is significant (more than a 10 percent decrease in performance in a week), reduce the degree of overload for a few days or switch to another activity. After the appraisal and tapering off, improvement is bound to follow. Don't be discouraged. Retrogression is fairly common.

Use and Disuse. The sixth principle of training is that of use and disuse. If you regularly use part of your body to perform a certain task, the efficiency of that part will remain the same or improve. Conversely, if you do not regularly use a part of your body, the efficiency of that part will degenerate. Muscles grow stronger when exercised; muscles that are underexercised lose strength. In short, use promotes function, while disuse may reduce the ability to function.

Skill. Much of the improvement that occurs during the beginning stages of exercising must be attributed simply to learning how to do the particular exercises properly. For example, the first time you try to do sit-ups, you may not even be able to do one. But at the end of the week you may be able to do 7 or 8. The improvement is due not so much to increased strength as to improved technique.

Individual Response Rates. Each person has his or her own rate of response to the training program. Occasionally, some people seem to arrive at a high level of conditioning long before others. The reason for this difference is not clear. It's probably due to several variables, a few of which may be: present physical condition; age; body type; weight; rest, sleep, and relaxation; nutrition; freedom from disease; proneness to injury; motivation; and the ability to learn new skills.

Stomach Exercises for Any Place and Any Time

Not everyone enjoys exercise. Some people avoid it like the plague and make excuses: "I don't have the time," or "It's too much hassle." Of course, even a dedicated exerciser may not be able to find the time to exercise every day. Travel schedules, domestic and social responsibilities, and long hours on the job cut into exercise time. But anyone can build stomach-flattening exercises into his or her daily routine.

It is possible for you to do certain exercises in very improbable places. The confirmed non-exerciser can exercise without going through the movements normally associated with traditional exercise programs. The man in an easy chair can actually stay there and still give his stomach a workout. The woman behind a desk can be strengthening her stomach muscles while the sales manager is telling her of his latest idea—and he won't notice a thing. There are exercises you can do during a few private moments in your office. Finally, there are also fat-burning Aerobic exercises that you can adapt to your daily routines.

Isometrics

Isometrics were first brought to public attention in 1953 by physiologists T. H. Hettinger and E. A. Mueller at the Max-Plank Institute of Dortmund, Germany. Hettinger and Mueller claimed that daily muscle-contraction routines of six to eight seconds each could increase strength by as much as five percent a week. Since that original report, new research has not only borne out the findings of Hettinger and Mueller but has also indicated that muscle contraction without movement has a definite place in therapy and physical rehabilitation.

Although the benefits of no-sweat isometric exercises have been blown all out of proportion by various advertising pitches (some ads falsely claim that it takes only three minutes of isometrics daily to achieve overall fitness), isometrics can be used to improve muscle tone and increase strength. Just remember that isometrics have severe limitations and should be used only when you are necessarily pinched for time. They never should be considered a substitute for a regular exercise program.

We must add a strong word of caution before you decide to engage in isometrics. Isometric exercises may be dangerous for heart patients. Dr. O. A. Matthews, of the University of Texas Southwestern Medical School in Dallas, found that 11 of 23 patients with arteriosclerotic heart disease developed arrhythmias during isometric exercise.

Furthermore, of 18 patients with valvular heart disease, five had arrhythmias during isometric exercise and two of three patients with myocardial disease developed arrhythmias during isometric exercise. He also found that 78 percent of the patients developed premature ventricular contractions; and 20 percent of the patients developed these during isometric exercise. He recommended that heart patients not engage in any type of isometric exercise. We agree with Dr. Matthews. If you have a history of high blood pressure or of heart disease, do not do the isometric exercises.

If you are sure you have neither high blood pressure nor heart disease, you can use the isometric exercises described below to supplement your CONSUMER GUIDE® Flatten Your Stomach program and to help you through rough spots in your schedule or your mental attitude.

Abdominal Compression

You can do this exercise in almost any situation that requires you to sit or stand for a period of time. Simply pull in your stomach muscles as far as you can, keep them in for six seconds, then relax. Repeat this several times.

Some typical situations for seated abdominal compression are while you are driving your car, talking on the phone, waiting for a movie to start, typing, and giving or taking dictation.

Standing abdominal compression exercises can be performed while you are brushing your teeth, waiting for a bus, standing in a ticket line, or riding an elevator (although you should also get off the elevator before your floor and walk at least part of the way up).

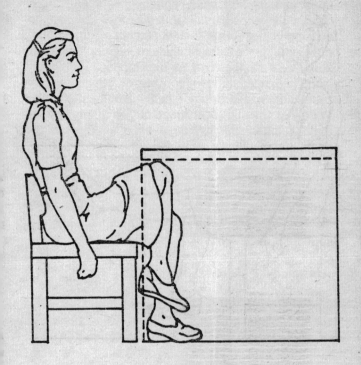

Raise The Desk

Sit in a chair and place both your legs under the desk. Raise one knee against the underside of the desk and attempt to lift the desk with your knee. Push for six seconds, then relax. Do this three times, then repeat the exercise using your other leg.

Raise The Desk

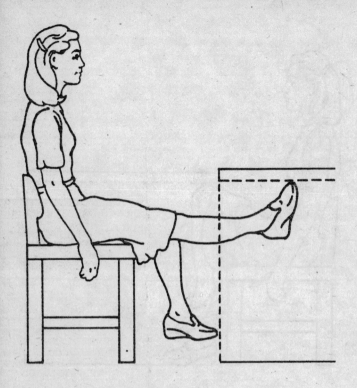

Another way to do this exercise is to sit in a chair so that both of your feet are under the desk. Raise your right leg, keeping your knee straight, until your toes touch the underside of the desk. Attempt to lift the desk with your straight leg. Push for six seconds, then lower your leg. Do this three times, then repeat the exercise with your other leg.

Raise The Desk

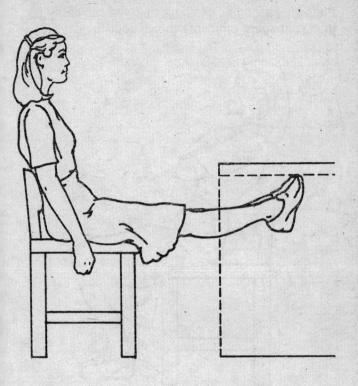

A third variation of Raise The Desk is to push against the desk with both feet simultaneously. Raise both legs, keeping your knees straight, and push against the bottom of the desk with your toes for six seconds. Lower your legs. Do this three times.

Exercises For Your Spare Moments

Following are some exercises that you can easily fit into your spare moments throughout the day.

Sit Back in a Chair

1. Sit on the edge of your chair, both feet planted firmly on the ground, arms across your chest.
2. Gradually sit back in your chair until your back almost touches the back of your chair. Hold this position for six seconds.
3. Gradually sit upward to a full sitting position.
4. Repeat as many times as possible.

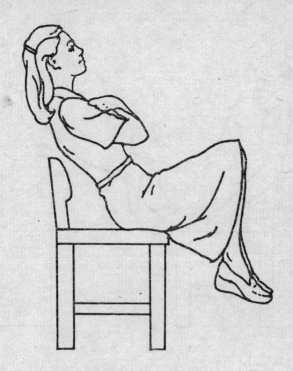

Sit Back, Raise Knee

1. Sit on the edge of the chair, both feet firmly on the floor, arms across the chest.
2. Gradually sit back in the chair until your back almost touches the back of your chair. As you sit back, lift your legs and feet off the floor by raising your knees upward. Your feet should be at least six inches off the floor.
3. Repeat as many times as possible up to 30.

Feet Off the Desk

1. Sit back in your chair with your feet on the desk.
2. Raise your feet off the desk and hold for six seconds.
3. Repeat as many times as possible, up to 30 times.

Exercises You Can Do When Your Office Door Is Closed

Following are some exercises you can do when you have free moments alone in your office. These aren't as subtle as the isometrics or the chair exercises described above, but they will help you trim your middle, and they don't require special clothing or equipment. For all of these exercises, start with four or five repetitions and gradually build up to 30. Choose those exercises that affect the areas of your body you think need the most work. Three to five of these exercises should be done daily.

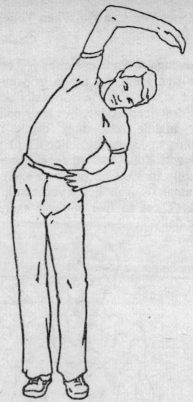

Standing Bend (Left and Right)

1. Stand erect with your feet spread shoulder-width apart, left hand on your hip, right arm extended at shoulder-height to the side.
2. Bend your trunk slowly to the left, simultaneously reaching slowly over and beyond your head with your right arm.
3. Return to starting position. Do this several times, then repeat, bending to the right and reaching with your left arm.

Body Twist

1. Stand erect, arms down at your sides.
2. Step forward with your left foot and twist your upper torso to the left, swinging both arms to your left as you do. All movements should be done slowly.
3. Return to starting position.
4. Step forward with your right foot and twist your upper torso to the right, swinging both arms to the right.
5. Return to the starting position.

Parallel Arm Swings (Golf Swings)

1. Stand erect, feet shoulder-width apart, arms relaxed at your sides.
2. Swing both arms together to the right and upward as high as possible. All movements should be done slowly.
3. Repeat to the other side to complete one full exercise.

Waist Exercises

Trunk Twister

1. Stand erect with your hands clasped behind your neck and your elbows drawn back.
2. Walk in place, using a high knee action.
3. As your right knee is lifted, turn your body to the right and touch your left elbow to your right knee. To do this, you will have to bend at the waist. When your left knee is lifted, you should touch your right elbow to your left knee.

Bend Left and Right

1. Sit in a chair, your feet comfortably on the floor, your left hand on your hip, your right hand extended at shoulder-height to the side.
2. Bend your trunk to the left and simultaneously reach over and beyond your head with your right arm.
3. Return to starting position.
4. Do this several times, then repeat on the other side. A variation is to place your hands behind you, keeping them there during the left and right movements.

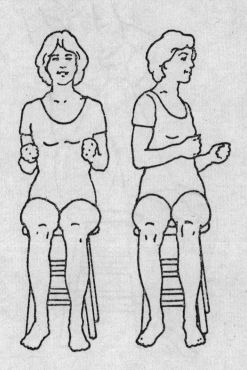

Sitting Twist

1. Sit erect in a chair, your arms bent and held chest high at your sides.
2. Twist your upper torso to your left.
3. Return to the starting position.
4. Repeat to the right.

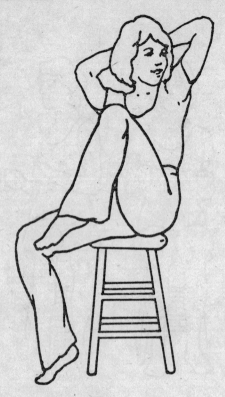

Sitting Trunk Twister

1. Sit in a chair, your hands clasped behind your head and your elbows drawn back.
2. Alternately raise your knees as high as possible.
3. As the right knee is lifted, turn your body to the right and touch your left elbow to your right knee. When the left knee is lifted, your right elbow should touch the left knee.

Abdomen Exercises

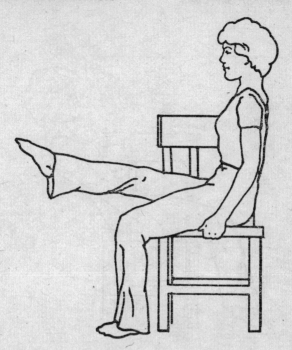

Sitting Single Leg Lifts

1. Sit in a chair and hold the sides of the chair for balance.
2. Straighten one leg, slowly raising it as high as possible.
3. Return to starting position. Do this several times, then repeat using the other leg.

Sitting Double Leg Lifts

Same as Sitting Single Leg Lifts, except raise both legs simultaneously.

Abdomen Exercises

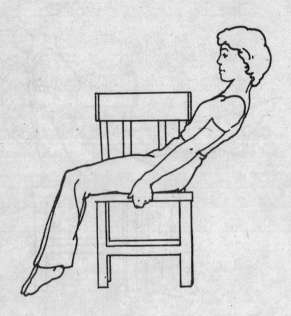

Curl-Down

1. Sit sideward in a chair, arms at your sides. You may hold onto the side of the chair with one of your arms for balance.
2. Slowly lower your upper body down to a 45° angle or until you feel a pull on your abdomen.
3. Hold this position briefly, then return to starting position.

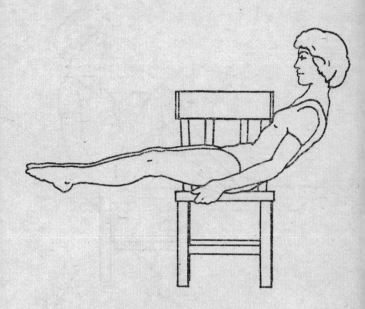

Curl-Up

1. Sit sideward in a chair, arms at your sides. You may hold onto the side of the chair for balance. Lower your torso and raise your legs until your body is parallel to the floor.
2. Curl your head and upper body upward and forward to about a 45° angle. Don't arch your back or jerk your body up.
3. Hold briefly and return to starting position.

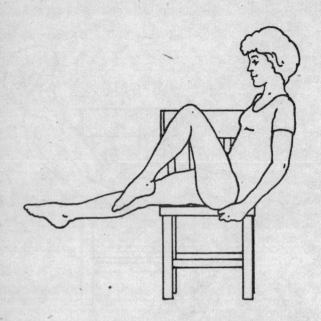

Bicycle Pumps

1. Sit sideward in a chair, arms at your sides. You
   may hold onto the side of the chair for balance
   if you wish.
2. Raise your legs off the floor and lean your upper body back slightly.
3. In this position, move your legs as though riding
   a bicycle. Be certain your legs are extended
   while performing the exercise. Keep your back
   slightly rounded.

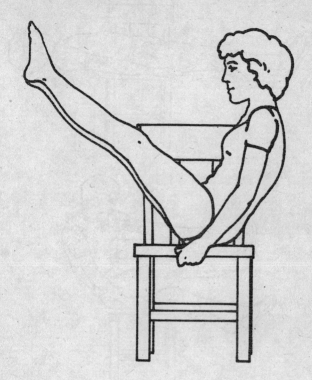

V-Seat

1. Sit sideward in a chair, arms at your sides.
2. Raise your legs off the floor and tilt your upper body backward slightly. Your body should form a V.
3. Hold for three to six seconds.
4. Return to starting position. Repeat several times. For variation, you can describe a figure 8 with your feet while in the V-Seat position.

Abdomen Exercises

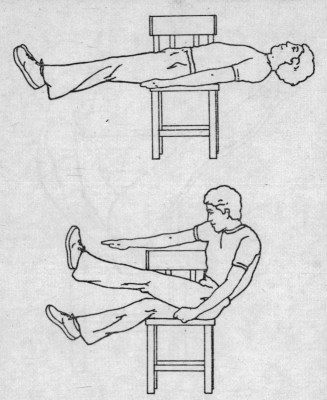

Sitting Alternate Toe Spikes

1. Lie on your back across the seat of a chair so that your body is parallel to the floor.
2. Slowly raise your upper body and simultaneously raise your left leg as high as possible. Touch your right hand to your left toe.
3. Return to starting position, then repeat using right leg and left hand.

Abdomen Exercises

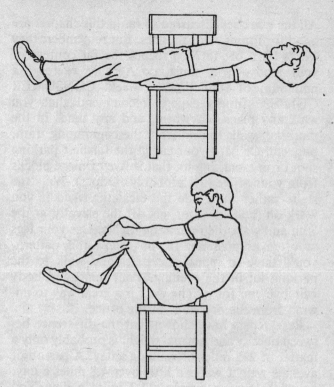

Up-Oars

1. Sit sideward in a chair, arms at your sides. Gradually lower your upper body so that it is parallel to the floor. Raise your legs so that they, too, are parallel.
2. Curl your upper body upward and simultaneously bend your knees.
3. Grab your hands around your shins.
4. Return to starting position.

Aerobic Exercise

All the exercises discussed so far in this chapter are good for toning your muscles. But remember: they won't burn off fat. To reduce the fat content of your body, you must do Aerobic exercise a minimum of four times a week. CONSUMER GUIDE® fitness experts recommend that you walk any place, anywhere, and any time. In the morning, walk to and from the commuting train, bus, etc. Or park your car in the farthest parking spot or in a parking lot that is five or more blocks from your office (it's probably cheaper). Walk the stairs rather than ride the escalator. And if you work on the 80th floor, get off the elevator at the 70th and walk the remaining flights. Use your legs as often as possible. If you follow this pattern, you'll have to repeat the stairs and walk to the parking lot in the evening. Your mind and body will love you for it. The walk is a great way to unwind from the pressures of the office.

Researchers have shown that the difference between obesity and normal weight is probably only a matter of 2½ miles of walking a day. A person of average weight walks a little over 4.8 miles a day; an obese person averages 2.2 miles a day. You could get that 2½ extra miles during your 40-minute lunch walk. If you do this regularly, you'll be amazed at the progress you'll make. Remember, for every mile you walk, you burn about 100 extra calories. That's about 10 pounds a year.

How to Keep from Getting Sore

Aches and pains—sure, we all have them at one time or another. But there is no reason to have more than your fair share. A little common sense and knowledge can go a long way toward reducing your chances of getting sore from exercising. There are four principles of painless exercising: (1) don't push yourself too hard; (2) always let your body adjust between exercises; (3) exercise on a comfortable surface; and (4) avoid exercises that may be harmful.

Don't push yourself too hard. Easy does it. Your stomach didn't become soft and flabby overnight. It took time. Restoration also takes time. If you approach your program too vigorously, you may show fast progress at first, but you're soon going to get sore and, perhaps, quit. But, if you follow the CONSUMER GUIDE® Flatten Your Stomach program, you'll keep your aches and pains at a minimum; you'll progress gradually and painlessly. Follow the guidelines we have built into this program and don't force yourself to go faster.

Let your body adjust between exercises. Give your body a respite between exercises. That is, don't do one abdominal exercise after another without a change of pace between. Get up and walk or jog a bit between exercises. If you do Sit-Ups and immediately follow them with V-Seats, then Up-Oars, and so on, you're headed for soreness. You'll also not be able to do the number of repetitions that you should do. By getting up and moving around, you burn a lot more calories, keep yourself at target heart rate, and eliminate local muscle fatigue.

Exercise on a comfortable surface. Do it on a mat. Most of the abdominal exercises that we have outlined are done while sitting on your rump. Unless you sit on a mat while doing the exercises, your tailbone may become sore. The skin over your tailbone may even get rubbed raw. If you don't have a mat to sit on, a towel folded four times will do. A carpet remanent or a piece of foam rubber will also work.

Avoid exercises that may be harmful. Unfortunately, the exercises that are most often recommended for stomach trimming are the exercises that can do more harm than good. These exercises are straight-leg sit-ups, toe touches, leg lifts, and back body arches. The following section discusses these exercises and the harm they can cause.

Harmful Exercises

Straight-leg sit-ups. Ask any physical educator which exercise is best to tone the abdomen, and he'll probably tell you the sit-up. He's right—up to a point. But there is a slight hitch. Sit-ups done in the classic way—with the ankles held down and the legs straight—may cause back problems. Sitting up with the legs straight causes the hip flexors, or the *iliopsoas* muscle (the muscle that runs from the spinal column to the thigh bone), to do most of the work. The hip flexor muscles are the strongest in your abdominal region. When these hip flexors are used, the pelvis is tilted forward and the muscles in the small of your back are contracted to form a swayback condition. Continuing to do this type of exercise will result in a shortening of the muscles in the lower back and thighs. It will also cause a constant forward tilt of the pelvis and will increase the lordotic curve in the lower back. This curve is where many back problems begin.

If you bend your knees when doing a sit-up, you place all the stress on the abdominal muscles. The hip flexors are immobilized. Therefore, the sit-up with the knees bent is a better exercise.

One more point: when doing sit-ups, do them in a curling motion. By doing so, you'll add to the stress on the abdominal muscles. Furthermore, there is less trauma to the lower back area.

Toe touching. Ask the same physical educator what's the second best exercise for stomach flattening, and he'll probably tell you toe touching. He's wrong. Toe touching does not do what most people expect. It doesn't trim the waistline. Gravity, not your abdominal muscles, pulls you down toward your feet. Toe touching is an exercise that strengthens the muscles of the low back. Unfortunately, toe touching can also aggravate these muscles. The action of bending forward and bouncing, in an attempt to touch the toes, forces the knees to be overextended. Consequently, tremendous amounts of pressure are placed on the lumbar vertebrae, a factor believed by many to result in low back complaints. Dr. Allan J. Ryan, editor of *Postgraduate Medicine* and *The Physician and Sportsmedicine*, has long advocated abolishing this exercise. So has Dr. W. H. Fahrni, orthopedics assistant, University of British Columbia Medical faculty. He's been critical of toe touching because of its possible detrimental effect on the discs of the vertebral column.

Some experts modify the exercise and say if a person curls down gradually and does not do an excessive amount of bobbing, they're not headed for any trouble. This modification may help, because most back ailments are caused by frequent and fast overstretching of the spinal extensors.

Another important consideration is that body mechanics experts tell us never to bend at our waists and lift with our backs. We're supposed to bend at our knees and lift with our legs. Doing this will avoid low back injury and pain. Why, then, do an exercise that contradicts this well-founded recommendation?

Leg lifts. Ask for a third stomach-flattening exercise from the physical educator, and he'll tell you leg lifts. Leg lifts are done by lying on your back, then raising your legs and holding your feet about six inches off the floor. This exercise has been criticized because it can increase the severity of low back pain and also aggravate lordosis, which is a precursor of low back trouble. Most physical fitness experts have placed restrictions on this exercise or have told people to avoid it completely.

The biggest problem with leg lifts is that the abdominal muscles usually aren't strong enough to hold your legs six inches off the floor for any length of time. Therefore, when you raise your legs, you are unable to keep your low back on the floor. As a result, there is a forward rotation of the pelvis. This rotation aggravates a low back condition. If you are able to hold your low back on the floor, this probably isn't much of a problem. But most people can't keep their backs flat on the floor. Furthermore, although leg lifts are often recommended for waist trimming, research has demonstrated that other forms of exercise are more effective.

Arching the back. There's one more exercise that needs comment. Some people think that stretching the abdominal muscles with back-arching exercises (called hyperextension of the back) is good for the abdominal muscles. It is not. To condition the abdominals, you must bring the upper body toward the legs. Arching the back does not strengthen the abdominals; it strengthens the low back and stretches the abdominals. Unfortunately, it also can distress the low back.

When you hyperextend (arch) your back, its natural curve is exaggerated. If done repeatedly, this can weaken the joints of your spine. Dr. Allan Ryan explains, "For the large number of individuals who have varying degrees of swayback with weakened abdominals, movements which overextend the back will only exaggerate the condition and at the same time place unnecessary strain on the lumbar joints. . . ."

Weakened abdominal muscles often allow a person's pelvis to rotate. As a result, hyperextension of the back occurs naturally, and the low back muscles become stronger than the abdominals. Any body arching increases this difference between the low back muscles and the abdominals and increases the forward curve of the spine. It is best in the beginning of any fitness program to emphasize abdominal work rather than low back work. After the abdominals are as strong as the low back muscles, low back exercises can begin.

No exercise program can be considered successful if its results include pain or injury. To avoid pain and injury, do the right exercises in the correct way.

A Special Word to Women

Many women feel concern about the effect pregnancy may have on their figures. They fear that pregnancy means the end of a youthful shape.

Much of the change in the appearance of a woman's body after pregnancy usually is due to sedentariness during the last few months of pregnancy. During the last three months, a woman finds she is uncomfortable or has difficulty breathing. So, she often tends to become less active. (Many women become less active even before that.) Furthermore, after the child is born, mother often sleeps when the baby sleeps so that she can be ready for action when the baby is awake; this, too, leads to a sedentary pattern of living. When a woman gets into these sedentary patterns before and after the child is born, her weight starts to escalate. As her weight increases, she becomes even less active, which means she gains still more weight.

And, of course, inactivity results in weakened abdominal muscles, which adds to both the feeling and appearance of "fatness."

None of this has to be the case, however. There are very few reasons why a woman shouldn't exercise both during and after pregnancy to keep her weight down and her abdominal muscles in condition. It's just a matter of taking a common-sense approach.

Exercise And Pregnancy

Research has shown that women who were physically fit before they became pregnant experience fewer complications during pregnancy and delivery than women who are not in good condition. In fact, athletes generally have quicker and easier deliveries than average women do.

A study conducted by W. A. Pfeifer revealed that the average duration of labor from rupture of membrane to delivery was 102 minutes for athletic women and 207 for nonathletes. Pfeifer noted that the reasons the athletes had shorter labors than the nonathletes were that the athletic women were more able to relax, had better breathing control, had *stronger abdominal musculature,* and had greater ability to reduce useless contractions of their arms and legs. In another study, Pfeifer found that athletes had fewer complications during pregnancy and 50 percent fewer Cesarean sections than the average.

If you are physically fit before becoming pregnant, you can probably continue to exercise during pregnancy. There have been many reports of women who have exercised right up until the last few days. One researcher has said that he knew a woman who jogged just three hours before the birth of her child.

We must make a strong point of caution, however. Although some women have competed in athletics during their sixth through ninth months of pregnancy and have experienced normal deliveries, you should consult your physician before engaging in any exercise. Bumps and falls can result in miscarriage. Also, pregnancy naturally increases the demand on your heart; the additional demand placed on it during exercise may be harmful if your heart has an undetected defect. Similarly, your kidneys and liver function with very little reserve capacity during pregnancy, and you must be careful not to overtax them.

Exercise can be an important factor in decreasing risks during pregnancy. But, the time to start exercising is before you get pregnant. It is then usually safe to continue to exercise while you are pregnant. But always talk with your doctor first.

Exercising After Childbirth

Most women are concerned about getting back into shape after the child has been born. General conservative medical practice indicates that if a pelvic examination reveals that everything is back to normal, you can return to a regular exercise program. Most obstetricians recommend resumption of regular exercise about six weeks after childbirth. Again, it is best to consult with your physician before attempting something too strenuous. Once you receive the go-ahead from your physician, we recommend that you do the following sequence of simple exercises to help regain your figure before resuming the CONSUMER GUIDE® program.

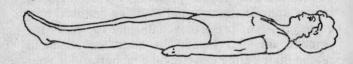

1. Lie on your back and take 5 deep breaths. Breathe from the abdomen.

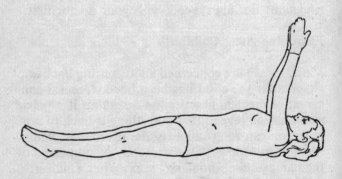

2. Lie on your back with your arms out at right angles to your body. Lift your arms, keeping them straight, and touch your palms together. Return to starting position. Do this five times.

3. Lie on your back with your knees bent. Raise your head off the floor so that your chin touches your chest. Do this 10 times.

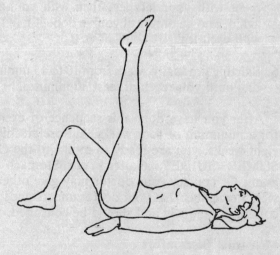

4. Lie on your back with your knees bent. Raise your left leg off the ground as high as possible. Keep the leg straight. Then lower the leg, making full use of the abdominal muscles. Repeat with the right leg. Do this 10 times.

5. Lie on your back with your knees bent. Raise your right knee, drawing the thigh down on your abdomen and chest, and the calf and heel against your thigh and buttock. Straighten your leg and lower it to the floor. Repeat the movement with your left leg, then with your right again, and so on, until you've done it five times with each leg.

6. Starting gradually, walk from 10 to 15 minutes a day until you reach at least 30 minutes.

After you have done this sequence of exercises for a minimum of four weeks, but preferrably for eight weeks, you are ready to return to the CONSUMER GUIDE® Flatten Your Stomach program. Of course, your doctor may give other advice. Remember that your doctor understands your condition uniquely and should be consulted.

Menstrual Discomfort

Some women experience levels of pain during menstruation that range from a few slight twinges in the abdomen and low back region to violent cramps, nausea, and headaches. This is known as dysmenorrhea, or painful flow. In most cases, exercise can greatly reduce such discomfort. A study conducted at the University of Michigan pointed out the importance of exercise in relieving dysmenorrhea. Eighty-seven percent of a group of freshmen who suffered moderate or severe cases of dysmenorrhea and then performed prescribed abdominal exercises for a minimum of eight weeks showed a decrease in severity of dysmenorrhea.

Gynecologists estimate that between 20 and 30 percent of dysmenorrhea cases are caused by such organic problems as infection, cysts, or endocrine imbalance. In such cases, exercise will not solve the problem directly. However, between 70 and 80 percent of the cases of dysmenorrhea are caused by poor posture, insufficient exercise, fatigue, improper diet, and weak abdominal muscles. In these cases, exercise can directly or indirectly relieve the discomfort.

Poor posture is often the result of weakened muscles in the shoulders, stomach, and back. Weak abdominal muscles simply need strengthening, and there is no better way to do it than through exercise.

Fatigue occurs when your need for physical activity exceeds your level of fitness. Women who are physically unfit experience fatigue more readily than women who exercise regularly. It has not been determined conclusively to what degree the fatigue-fighting benefits of exercise are physiological in origin and to what degree they are psychologically caused; in all likelihood, they are a result of both physiological and psychological factors.

Following is a series of exercises that can be effective in reducing dysmenorrhea. These exercises can help relieve the congestion in the abdominal area caused by poor posture, poor circulation, or poor muscle tone. They can also help relieve back and leg pain.

1. Mosher. Lie on your back with your knees bent, feet flat on the floor, and your right or left hand resting lightly on the lower abdomen. Slowly force your abdominal wall up against the hand as far as possible. Slowly contract the abdominal wall and relax. Repeat 10 times. Breathe normally throughout the movement.

2. Cat Exercise. Kneel on your hands and knees. Raise your back as high as possible, tucking your pelvic girdle under and contracting the abdomen. Relax. Repeat 8 to 10 times, maintaining rhythm throughout.

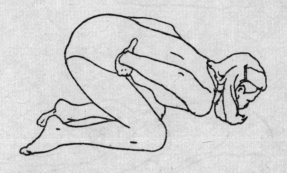

3. **Knee-Chest.** Kneel on all fours with your knees
   approximately 12 inches apart, your hips directly over your knees, and your chest as close to
   the floor as possible. Hold the position for three
   to five minutes. Slide forward into the prone
   position.

4. Thigh to Chest. Kneel with your knees about 12
   inches apart. Rest your chest and abdomen on
   your thighs, and place your hands back by your
   heels. Take three or four deep breaths. Keeping
   your chest and thighs in place, move your arms
   out in front of your head. Breathe three or four
   times, stretching your fingertips forward and
   pushing your hips backward with each inhala-
   tion. Relax after each exhalation.

5. Walk. It's a great tension reliever and great for circulation and weight control.

6. Follow the CONSUMER GUIDE® Flatten Your Stomach exercise program. It will tone up your stomach muscles.

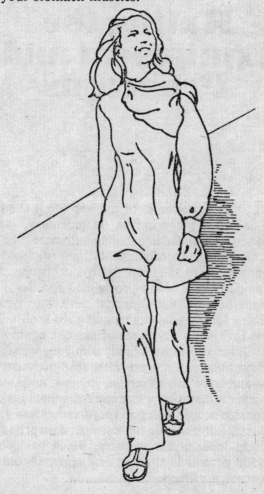

Rating the Equipment and Programs

One of the great ironies of modern life is the fact that exercise—the opposite of sedentary, push-button living—is itself becoming automated. In the past, the evangelists of physical fitness preached effort and sweat as the route to physical fitness. But now, a new breed of self-proclaimed apostles is offering a host of machines and devices to people searching for physical vitality and good health. The idea is inviting: a new piece of exercise equipment that will help you lose weight, trim your waistline, and condition your heart with absolutely no effort—an end to tiring exercise, jogging, and sweat.

The great majority of exercise equipment makers are reliable people with good consciences and good products. But it should not come as a surprise that a billion-dollar-a-year industry, which has grown over 500 percent in the past few years, should attract some profiteers.

Separating the good equipment from the worthless, or even harmful, is a tough assignment. A rule of thumb, however, seems to be that the greater the claims, the poorer the device.

As we said earlier, fat accumulates due to inactivity and overeating. The only way to lose weight and fat is to increase your activity level and decrease your food intake; your calorie outgo must exceed your calorie intake. So, devices that roll and massage you are not going to do any good as far as losing weight is concerned. Despite this fact, elaborate tables, couches, chairs, beds, cushions, belts, and small hand-held apparatus at prices ranging from a few dollars to several hundred dollars continue to be popular. Such devices do produce movement of your body, but it isn't you who are doing the moving!

Losing weight, reducing body fat, and flattening your stomach require effort on your part, not on a machine's. There is no other way; a company that claims otherwise is pulling your leg, because the only types of equipment that have been shown to help reduce body fat are those that allow you to maintain your pulse in the target range with continuous exercise. Such devices include treadmills, stationary exercise bicycles, and rowing machines. Furthermore, only the equipment with which you can perform exercises that place stress on your abdominal muscles, or cause the upper body to be flexed toward the legs, will help you flatten your stomach.

Nebulous Claims To Hook The Unwary

"Our device improves muscle tone." That is a commonly made advertising claim.

Muscle tone is the degree of contraction your muscles maintain while you are at rest. The degree of contraction of any muscle depends on the response of the muscle to your nervous system. The tone will vary depending upon such factors as whether you are lying down or standing up.

Manufacturers are hard pressed to prove that their devices improve muscle tone. It is not known whether exercise itself, let alone mechanical exercise, has an effect on muscle tone. Therefore, there is no reason to believe that the use of a vibratory abdominal belt, or a vibratory bed, pillow, or other device will "tone up" muscles so as to reduce girth.

Personal testimonial by a famous person is another questionable technique used to promote exercise devices for the stomach. Don't rely on such testimonials. Remember that the person generally is paid to make the testimonial.

Another popular advertising approach that should be regarded with suspicion is the type that announces that using a piece of equipment for three to six minutes a day will provide all the benefits of swimming a mile or jogging two miles. Such claims cannot be true unless using the equipment increases your pulse rate to what it would be if you were actually swimming or jogging, and keeps it there for as long as the actual exercise would. What's more, the product must force you to burn as many calories as the exercise and stress the same muscle groups to support the claims made for it. Besides, any product that would give you the equivalent exercise of jogging two miles or swimming a mile in a three- to six-minute period would probably be harmful.

"Spot reducing" is another favorite term used in advertising. It implies that it's possible to reduce the amount of fat at a particular part of the body by performing certain exercises. This is physiological nonsense.

Unfortunately, useless and falsely advertised exercise equipment has resulted in skepticism toward all such devices, even though some of them can help you.

The balance of this chapter evaluates two general types of equipment. One is the *passive* device—a machine that works on you. In other words, you allow yourself to be shaken, shocked, rolled, strapped, and girdled. The other is the *active* device— you work on the machine.

Passive Equipment

If you're already using the passive type of device, don't kid yourself into thinking you're getting much out of it. Such devices may relax you and may make you feel like a million dollars, but many authorities agree that such products make little, if any, contribution to fitness. The American Medical Association's Committee on Exercise and Physical Fitness, for one, is skeptical: "Effortless exercise . . . cannot benefit a person in any magical way."

If you're going to benefit from exercise, you must put effort into it. So don't be misled by health club claims that a machine is unique or approved by a doctor. Passive exercise equipment cannot help you become fit, nor will it roll off fat. But let's take a closer look.

Massage

To understand massage, let's quickly review

adipose tissue. The number of fat cells in your body is determined early in life, perhaps even before birth. Some researchers believe that the number of such cells may increase during an individual's first three years, while others suggest that the number may not stabilize until adolescence. In adulthood, it is the size—not the number—of fat cells that increases. When you are young and physically active, the fat cells are relatively low in fat content. But as you become more sedentary and burn off fewer calories, your cells fill up with fat—a special form of fat called triglyceride. Unfortunately, most of the fat cells seem to be located in the middle third of the body—the stomach area.

Exactly how fat gets into the fat cells has not been determined, but it is believed that the number of fat cells, the rate of fat circulation, enzyme action, and nervous and hormonal factors all play a role in depositing fat in the body. A blood vessel and a nerve are attached to each fat cell or group of fat cells; the nervous system can trigger the release of fat, which the circulatory system then distributes.

The precise way in which fat gets out of the cells is another unresolved issue, but, again, research points out that it involves a combination of factors, including the circulatory, nervous, endocrine, and muscular systems. A key element appears to be hormonal action.

Insulin and adrenalin are thought to play critical roles in fat synthesis (insulin) and fat dissolving (adrenalin). Insulin tends to increase appetite because it reduces blood glucose levels in the body. Adrenalin increases the blood glucose levels and encourages fat mobilization. Another hormone—a growth hormone—has the main metabolic function of increasing the rate of breaking down fat. Other research suggests that testosterone and corticoids also play an important role in fat deposition and removal.

Dr. Jerome Knittle, M.D., sums it up: "Hormonal actions can markedly affect adipose-cell size by virtue of their effect on metabolism and cellular proliferation." What all this means is that getting fat into and out of cells is the function of a complicated biochemical mechanism that involves almost every body system.

Massage has been defined as a "systematic manipulation of soft tissue of the body for therapeutic purposes." According to Dr. Miland E. Knapp, the effects of massage may be classified as "reflex" and "mechanical." Reflex refers to the pleasurable sensations felt with massage, which results in relaxed muscles and reduction of mental tension. Mechanical effects include improving the circulation of blood and lymph, stretching adhesions between muscle fibers, and mobilizing accumulations of fluid. But the effects of massage don't include reducing body fat; indications are that almost every system in the body, including the nervous, circulatory, endocrine, digestive, and muscular systems, is involved in getting fat in and out of the cells.

Unfortunately, there are many misconceptions about massage. Far too often, the teaching of massage has been done by people who know little about physiology. For example, one writer said, "Massage breaks down the fat so that it can be carried away by the bloodstream." No documentation is given for this kind of interpretation because there is none.

EVALUATION: Massage is not recommended for reducing body fat or weight because it cannot do so. It is not a substitute for active exercise. It can, however, be effective for the release of tension and relief of aching muscles.

Massaging Machines

Massaging machines include vibrators, rollers, and hydromassage (whirlpool) units of various types. Some devices are comfortable vibrating chairs, others are machines that perform kneading and stroking movements. There also are appliances that rely on revolving wooden rollers or vibrating belts to produce light stimulation to various body parts.

Such devices are often used in an attempt to massage flab away from the abdomen. Although such a device may help temporarily to relieve muscles that are sore due to unusual exercise for long periods of time, don't expect too much. Massaging machines offer no easy route to physical fitness. The late Arthur Steinhaus, Ph. D., demonstrated that mechanical vibrators are not a legitimate way to remove or redistribute body fat. He subjected 13 men (some markedly overweight) to a 15-minute period of vigorous vibration by a belt massager, with the belt placed around their abdomens. He found that they used up about 11.41 extra calories per 15-minute bout (about one twenty-third of an ounce of body weight). Steinhaus also measured blood fat levels and learned that there was no increase in the amount of fat circulating in the bloodstream. According to his calculations, one would have to use the vibrator 15 minutes a day for a full year to lose one pound of fat. (A 15-minute walk daily would take off 10 pounds a year!) His conclusion was that "the vibrator is not to be taken seriously as a device to assist in fat reduction or in shifting of fat deposits within the body."

Hydromassage Units

These may include portable or self-contained units whose purpose is to direct streams of water forcefully at the body. The water provides a massage, sometimes gentle and sometimes not so gentle. Some people claim that the devices help to redistribute fat. The fact, however, is that they have no real fitness value. They may be helpful in bringing temporary relief to minor aches. But they will not change body composition.

EVALUATION: Hydromassage (whirlpool) units are probably useless for weight reduction and muscular fitness.

Belt Vibrators

A belt vibrator is simply a motor-driven belt that is supposed to shake or vibrate fat off your body, often fat from around the waist. Belt vibrators are not effective because there is absolutely no evidence to support the contention that fat can be rolled, shaken, or vibrated off the body. They may be a nice way to relax, but they are a waste of money as far as reducing is concerned.

EVALUATION: Belt vibrators are probably useless for weight reduction and muscular fitness.

Roller Machines

These are the devices with a series of rollers that are

supposed to massage fat off the stomach. External massage will not remove fat. And, such machines can be dangerous for people with certain circulatory problems.

EVALUATION: Roller machines cannot help you reduce, and they may be dangerous.

The "Cellulite" Concept

In her book *Cellulite: Those Lumps, Bumps and Bulges You Couldn't Lose Before*, beauty expert Nicole Ronsard told the public that "orange peel fat—that ugly, bumpy type—is 'cellulite'." She described cellulite as fat that is trapped in the connective tissues and saturated with water and toxic waste. "Cellulite is that fat that you just can't seem to lose. . . . It is a gel-like substance made up of fat, water and waste, trapped in lumpy, immovable pockets just beneath the skin. These pockets of 'fat gone wrong' act like sponges that can absorb amounts of water, blow up and bulge out, resulting in ripples and flabbiness you see," she wrote.

Ronsard believes that cellulite is not simply fat, and that a low-calorie diet is no solution to the problem. She states that such a diet will decrease fat, but the cellulite bulges will remain. Cellulite experts claim that one needs a diet that "purifies the blood of excess water and toxic waste without forcing it to burn fat in unnecessary areas." These advocates also recommend a diet that consists of raw fruits and vegetables, low-fat foods, lean meats, plenty of water, yogurt, and brewer's yeast. The intake of salt is also reduced. In addition to the diet, they believe that exercise; massage; high-pressure water massage (squirting a hose on the fat area); relaxation; deep breathing; and overworking the kidneys, intestines, and sweat glands (which means sauna bathing and consuming lots of natural laxatives and diuretics), will remove cellulite.

CONSUMER GUIDE® fitness experts regard the cellulite concept as a dubious proposition, and our skepticism is shared by many experts in the field. Dr. Philip L. White, director of the AMA's food and nutrition department, calls cellulite a figment of Mme. Ronsard's imagination. Dr. Morton Glenn, past president of the American Nutritional Association, says, "There is no such thing in medical science." David Shepro, Ph. D., and Howard Knuttgen, Ph. D., of Boston University, are not so emphatic as White and Glenn but clearly have doubts. They question whether the cosmetic condition is unique, and whether it can be treated specifically. They also say that except for the high fees charged, they have no objection to the usual prescription for such treatment: plenty of exercise, a balanced diet, massage, sauna, and yoga. Although Shepro and Knuttgen doubt whether the treatment will cure cellulite, they point out that the treatment will not harm you.

CONSUMER GUIDE® fitness experts agree that people do have "orange peel fat," characterized by a dimpling of the skin. But why this happens to some people and not to others is unclear.

The Ronsard contention that cellulite is fat trapped in connective tissues may be based on outdated concepts. At one time, physiologists thought fat was passive in nature and not involved in the body's energy metabolism. According to Dr. H. E. Wertheimer, of the Hebrew University Hadassah School and one of the world's foremost authorities on adipose tissue, it was believed that the main function of fat was to insulate the body against heat loss and act as support for other tissue. He explains, however, that this thinking has changed. More recent evidence indicates that fat may be stored in two different types of adipose tissue—one that holds fat ready for a rather quick conversion into energy and a second type of tissue in which the fat is held for slower conversion. In either case, the fat does not remain in the cell for an extended period of time.

Orange peel fat appears primarily on inactive people, even people who have dieted for most of their life. It rarely is found on active people. The key seems to be activity.

EVALUATION: Cellulite is just plain fat that has accumulated near the surface of the skin. It is not yet known why the dimpling effect occurs in some people and not in others. Why this fat occurs only in certain body areas even has not been determined. CONSUMER GUIDE® fitness experts suggest that it occurs more often in women than in men because American women are encouraged to lead a more sedentary life, particularly during their teen-age and adult years, than are men.

The massage that cellulite people recommend may break tension, but it does not break down fat. And, the concept of "toxic gas" accumulation in connective tissue is not correct.

Several recommendations from the cellulite people are good—exercise, good nutrition, relaxation, and good elimination. For example, good elimination is essential in keeping the body's fluids at a proper level. Too much fluid may contribute to the "orange peel" effect.

Overall, the cellulite program is not recommended for reducing body fat on the stomach. If you want to get rid of that fat, including the orange peel kind, you must follow good dietary recommendations and engage in exercise that keeps your heart rate in the target range for 20 to 30 minutes four times a week.

Figure Wrapping

Figure wrapping comes in many packages. Some of the most popular include the "Shape Wrap," "Body Wrap," "Continental Miracle Wrap," "Swiss Trim," "Insta-trim," "Suddenly Slim," "Suddenly Slenda," and the "Benne Method" treatments. One of many ridiculous claims is that "You must lose four to twelve inches with the first treatment."

In a figure-wrapping treatment, you remove your clothing and are measured at predetermined locations on your body, a procedure that may be very difficult to duplicate at home. This is because you do not know the technique for arriving at a certain measurement (whether four inches from shoulder, three above the knee, etc.). Another trick that may be used is holding the tape measure in such a manner that the customer is not able to read it to verify the measurement recorded by an attendant.

After measuring, you are wrapped, mummy fashion, from neck to ankles in special tapes that have supposedly been soaked in a "magical solution." Parts of the body that do not need reducing may be omitted from the wrapping. Then, you don a rubberized sweat suit with elasticized cuffs and neck to prevent air circulation. Finally, covered by a blanket, you relax in a lounge chair and listen to music or watch television. At the end of an hour, the tapes and suit are removed, and you are remeasured.

Does this work? Dr. Ruth Lindsey concluded that it does not. Dr. Lindsey, professor of health and physical education and recreation at Oklahoma State University, working in cooperation with the American Medical Association and the U. S. Food and Drug Administration, conducted a survey of figure-wrapping salons. The results are disturbing. In the March/April 1972 issue of *Fitness for Living,* Dr. Lindsey stated that the treatment may be risky. She cites the dangers of dehydration and heat exhaustion. Also, the "magical solution" in which the wrapping tapes are soaked often contains aluminum sulfate, which can produce skin irritation as well as maceration (softening of the tissue itself.)

Dr. Lindsey goes on to describe how a variety of factors combine to create the illusion of real weight loss. Cold air may be used to constrict the saturated victim's superficial blood vessels, thereby creating a temporary reduction in his or her body measurements. The dehydration effect of the "magical solution" and the pressure from the wrappings may add to the apparent reduction of body size. But the changes caused by these factors are temporary at best. In a few hours, the victim is back to normal size.

Dr. Lindsey's conclusions are firm and negative: "There is no chemical substance known to science which can be applied to the body to produce a permanent effect and/or 'react with fat' to make it disappear. Aside from the possible health hazards . . . , it appears that the efficacy of such reducing treatment is highly questionable." Again, quite simply, she says, "There is no way to reduce weight or bulk except through exercise and diet control. There are no miracles. In the long run, from what we have found, figure wrapping doesn't work.''

EVALUATION: Figure wrapping does not work and can be dangerous.

Sweat Your Fat Off?

For years, sweating has been equated with weight loss, getting fit, and ridding the body of wastes. Nothing, however, could be further from the truth. The human body can be compared to an engine with a thermostat, except that the human thermostat cannot be turned off. The body produces heat in many ways—for example, by cell activity, muscular activity, digestion of food, and production of hormones. It also picks up heat from rays of the sun bouncing off sand or snow. Whatever the source, the body must protect itself from accumulating too much heat. Under normal conditions, heat is lost in a number of ways—through the skin, through sweat, through the lungs, and through waste.

During exercise, the situation changes and sweat becomes the most important element in keeping the body cool. For sweat to produce a loss of heat, it must evaporate. As it does so, it cools the blood close to the surface of the skin, which then returns to the body's inner-core tissues. At the same time, the interior blood carries heat from the deeper tissues toward the skin, where the heat can be lost to the environment. During exercise, circulation is speeded up and makes this heat exchange more efficient.

In an atmosphere with low humidity, sweat will evaporate very quickly into the dry air. Likewise, when a breeze is blowing, the currents will aid evaporation. But if the humidity is high (the air is saturated with water), the atmosphere cannot handle the sweat so it simply drips off your body. As a result, the blood near the skin's surface is not cooled, the temperature of the core tissue is not lowered, and the body temperature continues to rise.

Heat exhaustion is the body's reaction to a sustained period of inhibition of sweat evaporation. The blood rushes quickly to the body surface in an effort to carry the core heat to the skin where sweat evaporation can disperse it. As the blood flows to the surface capillaries, blood pressure drops. At the same time, blood volume is reduced because some of the liquid does pass into the skin cells and evaporates as sweat. As the heart becomes less able to maintain blood pressure, there is a slow-down in circulation. The core heat no longer escapes the body, and heat exhaustion occurs.

The general signs of heat exhaustion are profuse sweating, moist skin, and a rapid pulse. The victim is usually very uncomfortable and gasps for breath. Collapse and loss of consciousness may follow. The victim needs fluids and rest; recovery is usually rapid.

Dehydration exhaustion occurs when a person does not take in enough water while exercising. During extremely strenuous exercise, when one is sweating considerably, the person can lose about eight quarts of water in 90 minutes. Even during moderate exercise, water loss can be around three quarts in 90 minutes, which is virtually impossible to replenish in 90 minutes. Consequently, there's a decrease in blood volume. A stimulus is sent to the hypothalamus which, in turn, signals the release of a hormone to slow down the body's production of urine so that water is conserved.

If profuse sweating continues and the fluid lost is not replaced, heat stroke develops. Heat stroke is characterized by a rising temperature and very dry skin. Unless the body temperature is promptly reduced, permanent damage to the cells of the brain will occur—and very probably death. This is a medical emergency, and a doctor must be called immediately.

How does heat stroke develop? It begins with a rise in skin temperature, followed by sweating and expansion of the blood vessels (vasodilation). As the temperature continues to rise, further vasodilation and sweating take place. Soon the point is reached where sweating efficiency decreases. When that happens, the blood is no longer cooled adequately, the core temperature rises, sweating ceases altogether, and heat stroke occurs.

The loss of water is only part of the problem. With heavy sweating, the body also loses many electrolytes (sodium, chloride, and potassium). A prolonged loss of electrolytes and water may cause nausea, diarrhea, and fatigue, and it may impair kidney functioning to the point where kidney tissue damage occurs.

Misconceptions about the relationship of sweating to fat and weight loss around the middle have lead to some controversial practices. Here are a few of them.

Nonporous And Heavy Sweat Suits

Walk into any gymnasium and you'll find people wearing rubberized or other nonporous sweat suits designed to enclose the body in a hot environment.

Users tend to think that if they continue to exercise this way their paunches will go away. But all they're getting is a dangerous increase in body temperature. The suit traps the heat given off by the body, and sweat cannot evaporate. As a result, body temperature starts to rise very rapidly and heat exhaustion, dehydration exhaustion, or heat stroke can occur.

Of course, people wear such outfits with the idea of losing weight. After a good workout, the individual may discover that he has lost three to five pounds or even more weight. But this weight loss is only temporary. They lost water, not fat. As soon as the person drinks liquid, he or she will put the weight back on. To add to the problem, the nonporous sweat suits cause a strain on the heart and blood vessels of the body. It makes the heart work harder under very undesirable conditions. In exercise, you can control the pumping of the heart by simply stopping whatever you're doing. But when you overload your heart by overheating, such as you would with a rubberized sweat suit, there's no way you can stop the excess sweating except by immersing yourself in very cold water.

EVALUATION: CONSUMER GUIDE® fitness experts condemn the use of nonporous or extremely heavy sweat suits. Such garments do not help flatten your stomach. Worse, they prevent the body from cooling itself, and the consequences can be disastrous.

Steam Rooms

Steam rooms are popular in many health clubs. The temperature in a steam room is maintained at 110° to 130°F. Since the humidity is also very high, a person who sits in the steam room will, of course, sweat profusely. But due to the high humidity, sweat cannot evaporate and have a cooling effect on the body. As a result, body temperatures can rise to dangerous levels. Clayton R. Myers, Ph. D., Lawrence Golding, Ph. D., and Wayne Sinning, Ph. D., say that "there is growing concern among physicians that . . . steam booths may be detrimental to health. Heat stress is not tolerated well by most middle-aged people. Heat exposure can lead to heat exhaustion. The dangers of heat exposure are increased if an individual enters the bath after exercise, when the body is trying to reduce its temperature."

EVALUATION: The steam room makes no contribution to fitness. And, CONSUMER GUIDE® fitness experts regard steam rooms as detrimental to health.

Saunas

Many claims have been made for the sauna. The great majority have appeared in newspapers, popular magazines, and in articles thin in research but fat with personal testimonials. Claims have also been made, of course, by sauna manufacturers. Two are that sauna bathing will cause a loss of weight and possibly a loss of body fat. We've already said that the only way to lose weight is to burn off more calories than you take in. Sitting in a hot sauna just does not burn off a significant number of calories. The weight lost in such a hot environment is water—not fat tissue. You may be three pounds lighter after the sauna bath, but you'll gain it back almost as soon as you eat or drink.

EVALUATION: The sauna will not flatten your stomach. It may, however, help you relax and "feel good."

Inflatable Garments

Rubberized sweat belts, girdles, and Bermuda shorts were once the rage. Such garments promised to take off up to 10 inches from around your waist in two weeks without dieting. Many people were convinced these products worked. They measured their waists, donned the inflatable garments, and did the prescribed exercises. After several minutes or hours, they took off the items and remeasured themselves. Lo and behold, they were indeed slimmer. But if they had measured themselves again a few hours later, they would have found they were back to their old size.

The reason they temporarily lost inches of girth was that the garments generated intense heat, and the cells directly underneath lost a large amount of water. The cells did "shrink" in size, but there was no real loss of tissue—only water. As the individual took in food or liquids, the cells regained the water they had lost and the wearer "regained" the inches.

In short, the theory of losing inches using an inflatable outfit is bunk. Research supports this stand. Researchers conducted a study in which they compared the weights and measurements of several groups of people. Some wore inflatable garments, some did not, and some were on a low-calorie diet. All subjects performed comparable exercise routines. The only significant difference among the groups after the exercise and diet regimens was a greater loss of weight among those who had dieted.

The conclusion was that "inches can be lost using an inflatable apparatus only if the user is on a 900-1,000-calorie-per-day diet."

Clayton Myers, Ph. D., reached similar conclusions. "There is no evidence that (sauna belts) will contribute to any fat reduction," he said. "A recent Federal Trade Commission decision has restricted advertising these devices since the evidence in support of these claims was insufficient."

For the most part, such devices are not dangerous. But it is conceivable that a person with high blood pressure, coronary artery disease, or extreme obesity may experience some problems because these garments can cause excessive constriction of the blood vessels. And, this can be dangerous.

EVALUATION: The inflatable garment is a waste of money. It's hokum.

Active Equipment

There are hundreds of active exercise devices on the market. These are devices that require the user to do the work. CONSUMER GUIDE® fitness experts provide some guidelines for evaluating such equipment. Not all of the equipment is designed specifically for trimming the waistline. Some may be used for other purposes, such as the development of strength. But here we only evaluate the equipment in terms of their aid in flattening your stomach.

Keep in mind that it is not necessary to purchase any of these devices. You can flatten your stomach following the program outlined in this book. But people may wish to use some of these exercise devices to begin a fitness program, exercise specific muscle groups, or compensate for orthopedic problems.

Motorized Treadmills

The motorized type of treadmill has a motor-driven belt that forces you to walk (or run) in place on the belt at a preselected speed. On many machines, the incline can be adjusted to simulate walking or running uphill.

The motor-driven treadmill can be an excellent piece of equipment for reducing body fat and weight. It is expensive, however, and difficult to store. With some larger models, adequate headroom can be a problem.

EVALUATION: Although an excellent piece of equipment, a motorized treadmill is quite expensive and can be boring to use. But it can help you reduce your body fat, provided that you use it four times a week and work at your target heart rate.

Non-Motorized Treadmills

Non-motorized treadmills operate on a different principle than motor-driven models. On machines without motors, your feet cause the belt to move. A flywheel keeps the device's belt moving at a constant speed. These machines are much less expensive than the motor-driven ones.

EVALUATION: The non-motorized treadmill is recommended for people who find it difficult to exercise outdoors. It can be used to reduce body fat, provided you confine your efforts to walking on it four times a week. It is not recommended, for running, because it can cause foot irritation.

Stationary Bicycles

Stationary bicycles are bicycle-like devices that remain stationary as you pedal them. They come in different sizes and styles. Some are motorized; others are non-motorized. Those without motors resemble an ordinary bicycle except for the lack of a rear wheel. The chain from the pedal sprocket goes to the front wheel, which turns as you pedal. Most have a knob that allows you to adjust pedal resistance by increasing or decreasing the pressure of the brake shoes on the front wheel.

Non-Motorized Bicycles

Non-motorized stationary bicycles are good devices for reducing body composition, especially for cardiac patients who need a precise measurement of the amount of work they've done. The bicycle should have a means of indicating the amount of resistance on the wheel.

EVALUATION: The non-motorized bicycle is a good product for reducing body fat in the stomach area.

Motorized Bicycles

The motorized stationary bicycle operates on a different principle. The motor turns the pedals at a preset rate. As a result, your legs are not required to do the work. The motor also causes the device's handlebars to move forward and backward, and the seat to move up and down.

Most motorized bicycles are probably overrated. While it is possible to get a target heart rate exercise if you work against the machine, little benefit is derived if you allow the machine to do the work. This type of device also is usually cumbersome and uncomfortable. And, it is difficult to measure the amount of work done.

EVALUATION: The motorized bicycle is not recommended. We believe that you can obtain at least the same benefits from a non-motorized bicycle at one-fifth the cost.

Rowing Machines

A rowing machine is a device designed to simulate the action of rowing a boat. It has a seat that moves along a steel frame as you exercise by moving the oars.

This is a moderately expensive device that is good for weight control. Because it forces you to use some of the abdominal muscles, it's probably an effective piece of equipment for flattening your stomach. There is, however, one negative aspect. The machine is not recommended for people with heart disease problems because extensive use of the upper body may cause blood pressure to rise excessively.

EVALUATION: Although the rowing machine is recommended to the general public as a good product for flattening your stomach, it is not recommended for use by individuals with high blood pressure or for heart disease.

Creeping Device

The creeping device is a compact unit on which two hand carriages and two knee carriages slide back and forth on tracks. The carriages are linked together so that all four move in unison. To exercise, you place your hands and knees on the carriages and move them back and forth as though you were creeping. Originally, it was designed to help children and adults improve their coordination, but more recently the manufacturer has claimed it can reduce body fat.

Although this is probably an effective way to burn calories and lose weight, the creeping device can be extremely boring to use. It is also expensive.

EVALUATION: The creeping device is a good piece of equipment to reduce body fat, but it's application is quite limited.

Exercise Wheel

An exercise wheel resembles a wheel from a small wagon or lawnmower. A dowel protrudes from each side. To exercise, you get into a creeping position, resting on your knees, and place your hands on the protruding dowel. Then you extend your body as far out as possible, pushing the wheel. Once you are extended as far as possible, you return to the starting position. This maneuver is to be repeated, and the exercise is supposed to trim your waistline.

EVALUATION: The exercise wheel is not recommended. It places you in an uncomfortable position and can be harmful to the lower back.

Rubber Stretchers

Rubber stretchers are highly elastic pieces of rubber with loops at each end. To use the device, you grip the loops with your hands and stand on the middle part of the stretcher. A series of exercises are then performed.

A rubber stretcher can develop strength in specific muscles, but it is of questionable value to adults who are interested in flattening their stomachs. The biggest drawback is that it doesn't allow any leeway for differences in strength. A very weak person may be unable to stretch the device or a very strong person may find it is much too easy to use.

EVALUATION: Rubber stretchers are not reccommended.

Body Trimmers

Body trimmers are pulley and rope systems that are attached to a door or a wall. You lie flat on the floor with your feet and hands attached to the ropes. As you move a leg forward, an arm will be pulled forward and vice versa.

Body trimmers use one set of muscles to work against another set. If they are properly used, an individual can regulate the resistance and perhaps derive some benefit.

EVALUATION: Body trimmers are not recommended. Calisthenics can produce better results at no cost.

Jump Ropes

Jump ropes come in a variety of styles and are made of cotton, nylon, polyethylene, leather, or hemp. Some have handles or weighted ends. Some come packaged with instruction booklets.

A jump rope is an excellent piece of exercise equipment, provided it is used regularly. Some people, however, believe that only a few minutes of rope skipping will produce significant results. This isn't true. To reduce body fat, you must exercise at your target heart rate level for a minimum of 30 minutes, four times a week.

EVALUATION: A jump rope is an excellent piece of equipment and there's no need to buy one. A homemade one will do.

Exer-Genie, Apollo Exerciser, Exer-Gym

The designs of such products as the Exer-Genie, Apollo Exerciser, and Exer-Gym are similar. At the top of a shaft enclosed in a casing is a metal loop or eye. A nylon line leads out of the shaft through the loops; a handle is attached to each of the two ends of the line. Resistance, preset by revolving the casing around the shaft, is achieved by friction from the movement of the specially braided-like winding around the shaft. It can be varied from free movement through maximum effort for individual exercises. The amount of line passing over the shaft determines the approximate resistance in pounds of pull, indicated on the calibrated chart that reflects an average resistance in sample testing. The Exer-Genie, Apollo Exerciser, and Exer-Gym devices usually come in a kit that includes the device itself, an instructional booklet, carrying case, handles, a foot board, and other materials. Additional materials, including a cassette tape, workout charts, and extra nylon cord and straps, may be purchased. Various exercises are suggested in the booklet and workout plans are given for developing various parts of the body.

These products are primarily designed for developing muscle strength and endurance. They are really not designed for reducing body composition and do very little to trim the waistline. In addition, poundages indicated on the devices are estimates. Exer-Genie is available from Exer-Genie, Inc.; Apollo Exerciser from the Physical Fitness Institute of America; and Exer-Gym from Exer-Gym.

EVALUATION: These products are not recommended for flattening your stomach.

Sit-A-Shape

The Sit-A-Shape, a gadget that can be attached to the bottom of most doors, is designed to hold your feet in position for sit-ups. Under no circumstances should this device be used while doing sit-ups with the legs straight, because it will probably aggravate the lordotic curve and cause back pain. You can use it when doing sit-ups with the knees bent, provided you use a curl-up movement. Sit-a-Shape is available from Sears.

EVALUATION: This is an acceptable product, provided the exercise is done with the knees bent.

Abdominal Board (Incline Board)

The Abdominal Board is a gadget designed to strengthen abdominal muscles. The advantage of this product and some other variations is that you can perform sit-ups when your feet are elevated one, two or three feet higher than your head. The foam-padded plywood board is about 84 inches long and 18 inches wide. It has a strap to hold your feet down. The Abdominal Board is available from Wolverine Sports.

EVALUATION: This type of exercise device is satisfactory provided sit-ups are performed with the knees bent.

Weighted Shoes And Vests

Weighted shoes and weighted vests can be convenient accessories when you combine weight training with Step 4 of the CONSUMER GUIDE® Flatten Your Stomach program. The advantage that weighted garments, such as shoes and vests, have over makeshift weights is that you don't have to hold them in place while you exercise.

Weighted shoes are usually attached to the feet with straps. Plates are then attached to the shoes to bring the shoes up to the desired poundage.

Vests are usually made of lightweight fabric and have pockets sewn on the outside. Metal weights are inserted into the pockets. You can regulate the weight of the vest by adding and removing weights from the pockets.

Mail-Order Suppliers

The following companies sell exercise equipment by mail. Write for information and/or catalogs.

Bell Foundry Company
5310 Southern Avenue
South Gate, CA 90280

Cran Barry, Inc.
2 Lincoln Avenue
Marblehead, MA 01945

Exer-Genie, Inc.
P.O. Box 3320
Fullerton, CA 92634

Exer-Gym
P.O. Box 100
Opelika, AL 36801

Flaghouse, Inc.
18 West 18th Street
New York City, NY 10011

Gopher Athletic Supply Co.
2125 NW 4th Street
Box O, Owatonna, MN 55060

GSC Athletic Equipment
600 North Pacific Avenue
P.O. Box 1710, San Pedro, CA 90733

Jayfro Corp.
P.O. Box 400
Waterford, CT 06385

Mini-Gym, Inc.
Box 266
Independence, MO 64051

Montgomery Ward & Co., Inc.
535 W. Chicago Avenue
Chicago, I L 60607

Passon's, Inc.
1017 Arch Street
Philadelphia, PA 19107

Physical Fitness Institute of America
851 Lake Shore Blvd.
Incline Village, NV 89450

Porter Equipment Co.
9555 Irving Park Rd.
Schiller Park, IL 60176

Professional Gym, Inc.
805 Cherokee
Marshall, MO 65340

Program Aids, Inc.
161 MacQuesten Parkway
Mount Vernon, NY 10550

Sears Roebuck And Co.
Sears Tower
Chicago, IL 60684

Todd-Phelps
1945 Palmer Avenue
Larchmont, NY 10538

U. S. Games, Inc.
Box EG 874
Melbourne, FL 32935

Weider Health And Fitness, Inc.
21100 Erwin Street
Woodland Hills, CA 91364

Wolverine Sports
745 State Circle
Ann Arbor, MI. 48104

York Barbell Company, Inc.
P.O. Box 1707
York, PA 17405

Appendix A:

Warming Up and Cooling Down

Warm-Up Exercises

These exercises are to be done before each exercise session in the CONSUMER GUIDE® Flatten Your Stomach program. They will loosen the muscles, tendons, and ligaments of your legs and neck. They will prepare your body for the more vigorous exercises to come. Do the warm-ups in the order listed here and follow them with a period of walking.

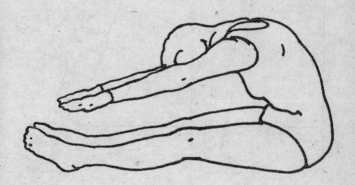

Sitting Toe Touches

1. Sit on the floor with your legs extended in front of you, feet together.
2. Reach for your toes with both hands, and bring your forehead as close to your knees as possible.

Calf Tendon Stretches

1. Stand two to three feet from a wall.
2. Lean forward and place your palms against the wall at eye level. Keep your body straight.
3. Keep your hands against the wall and your feet flat on the floor. Move your feet backward until you feel the muscles of your calves stretching.

Sprinter

1. Assume a squatting position and place your hands on the floor ahead of your feet.
2. Extend one leg backward as far as possible.
3. Hold this position for a few seconds, then repeat with the other leg.

173

Warm-Up Exercises

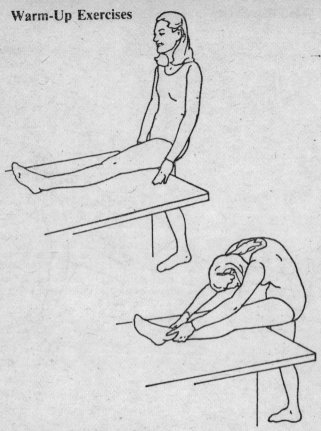

Standing Leg Stretches

1. Find a table about three feet high. Place one foot on the table and extend your leg so that the knee is straight and the leg is parallel to the floor.
2. Slowly extend the fingertips of your hands toward the foot that is on the table.
3. Try to touch your forehead to your knees.
4. Repeat with the other leg.

Head Flexor

1. Assume a standing position, your arms relaxed at your sides.
2. Slowly lower your chin to your chest, drawing your chin as far down as possible.
3. Slowly tilt your head backward as far as possible.

Neck Turns

1. Turn your head slowly to the left and look over your left shoulder.
2. Turn your head slowly to the right and look over your right shoulder.

Cool-Down Exercises

These exercises should be the last ones you do at each exercise session. They will help stretch your muscles, tendons and ligaments, and prepare your body for normal activity. Do the cool-downs in the order listed here.

Cool-Down Exercises

Calf-Achilles Stretch

1. Stand a few feet from a wall and rest your forearms on it. Place your forehead on the backs of your hands.
2. Move your right foot toward the wall, bending your knee as you do so and keeping your foot flat on the floor. Also keep your left leg straight, your left heel on the floor, and both feet pointed toward the wall.
3. Continue to move your right foot toward the wall until you feel the muscle of your left calf stretching.
4. Bend your left knee.
5. Hold this position for a few seconds. As you hold, you should feel the achilles tendon above your left heel stretching.
6. Repeat the exercise with the other leg.

Cool-Down Exercises

Side Stretch

1. Stand with your feet shoulder-width apart. Keep your legs straight.
2. Place your right hand on your right hip and extend your left arm above your head.
3. Slowly bend to the right. Hold this position for several seconds, then repeat on the other side.

Cool-Down Exercises

Shoulder Stretch

1. Lay your forearms on top of your head and grasp your right elbow with your left hand.
2. Slowly pull the elbow behind your head. Don't force it.
3. Hold this position for a few seconds, then switch arms and repeat.

Spinal Stretch

1. Sit on the floor with your legs straight out in front of you.
2. Keep your right leg straight and place your left foot on the other side of your right knee.
3. Twist your upper body to the left.
4. Place your right elbow against the outside of your left knee and, with your right hand, grasp your right leg near the knee.

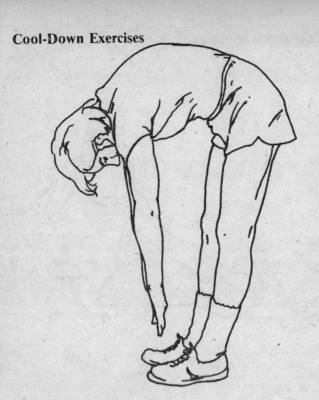

Back Stretch

1. Stand erect, feet shoulder-width apart.
2. Bend forward slowly from the waist. Relax your arms, shoulders, and neck.
3. Bend until you feel a slight stretching in the backs of your legs.
4. If you don't touch the floor, place your hands on the backs of your legs (this will give you support).
5. Hold this position for several seconds. When you straighten up, be sure to bend your knees to take the pressure off your low back.

Appendix B:

Alternate Exercises

You may substitute any of the following four exercises for walking in place during the CONSUMER GUIDE® Flatten Your Stomach program. NOTE: Don't use these exercises as alternates to jogging in place or stair climbing. The jogging and stair climbing segments of the program are essential for maintaining your target heart rate.

Fitness Lope

1. Stand erect and relaxed.
2. Kick your legs alternately to the sides. Stay on your toes, hopping as your weight shifts from one leg to the other.
3. Continue for the specified time.

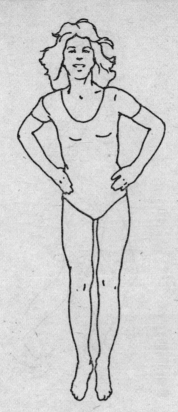

Toe Hops

1. Stand erect, your feet close together and your hands on your hips.
2. Spring lightly from your toes into the air.
3. Land on your toes and spring immediately back up. Don't touch your heels to the floor.
4. Continue hopping for the specified time.

Alternate Exercises

Stride Hops

1. Stand erect, hands on your hips, left foot forward in a striding position.
2. Lean forward slightly. Hop up and reverse the positions of your feet. For rhythm and balance, be sure you hop from both feet at the same time and land on both feet at the same time.
3. Immediately repeat the movement from the reversed position.
4. Continue in succession for the specified time.

Jumping Rope

Good form while jumping is important. You should remain relaxed. Keep your body erect and look straight ahead while you are jumping. Land on the balls of your feet. Hold the rope at about hip level and use as little arm movement as possible to keep it moving. Jump on a soft surface to avoid injuring the balls of your feet.

Consumer Guide®
Program Log
and
Progress Record

Keeping a daily log of your exercises and activities serves several good purposes. For one, it keeps you focused on the program. You're less likely to fudge when you've committed yourself not only to doing the exercises but to recording what you've done, as well. Another important reason for record keeping is that it gives you information about yourself that helps you adjust the program for maximum benefit. For example, you might discover that Mondays are your "bad" days. A glance at the log for several weeks might show that you don't get your heart rate in the target range on Mondays. Maybe that's a day on which you should jog or play raquet ball, instead.

We've set up a 20-week log for you to use with the CONSUMER GUIDE® program. In the log, you should note the Step and Level you're at in the program and your heart rate during that particular session. You should also note any exercises you did that day that aren't part of the program, such as those from the chapter "Exercises for Any Place and Any Time." Then, make a note of any special activities you may have engaged in, such as walking or tennis, and the distance or length of time you performed them.

Logging activities that aren't actually part of the CONSUMER GUIDE® program, but that have a bearing on your overall fitness, is another aid in tailoring the program to your unique situation. For example, a glance at the log and a monthly progress chart (which we talk about below) might tell you that after you stopped bicycling in November, you didn't lose as much weight as you did in October. So, maybe you ought to add some time to the jogging-in-place portion of the program or engage in some other Aerobic activity.

We've also included monthly progress record charts in the Log. On these charts you will record the vital statistics—weight, waist, any changes that may have occurred in your appearance, and so on. As we've said before, don't expect overnight miracles. A good look-over once a month is just enough to be encouraging.

On the day you begin your CONSUMER GUIDE® Flatten Your Stomach program, fill out the chart below. It will give you a reference point from which to gauge your improvement during the coming months.

Date: _____

My waist size: _____

My chest size: _____

My weight: _____

My body type (endomorph, ectomorph, or mesomorph): _____

Results of pinch test: _____

Results of poke test: _____

Number of sit-ups: _____

What I'd like to change about what I see in the mirror (sagging belly, protruding stomach, etc.): _____

My waist size should be: _____

My weight should be: _____

My target heart rate and range: _____

WEEK 1

	Step, Level	Heart Rate	Other Exercises	Activities
Monday				
Tuesday				
Wednesday				
Thursday				
Friday				
Saturday				
Sunday				

WEEK 2

	Step, Level	Heart Rate	Other Exercises	Activities
Monday				
Tuesday				
Wednesday				
Thursday				
Friday				
Saturday				
Sunday				

WEEK 3

	Step, Level	Heart Rate	Other Exercises	Activities
Monday				
Tuesday				
Wednesday				
Thursday				
Friday				
Saturday				
Sunday				

WEEK 4

	Step, Level	Heart Rate	Other Exercises	Activities
Monday				
Tuesday				
Wednesday				
Thursday				
Friday				
Saturday				
Sunday				

MONTH 1 Progress Record

Waist: _____

Chest: _____

Weight: _____

Results of pinch test: _____

Results of poke test: _____

Number of sit-ups: _____

Changes in appearance: _____

How I feel: _____
_____
_____
_____

WEEK 5

	Step, Level	Heart Rate	Other Exercises	Activities
Monday				
Tuesday				
Wednesday				
Thursday				
Friday				
Saturday				
Sunday				

WEEK 6

	Step, Level	Heart Rate	Other Exercises	Activities
Monday				
Tuesday				
Wednesday				
Thursday				
Friday				
Saturday				
Sunday				

WEEK 7

	Step, Level	Heart Rate	Other Exercises	Activities
Monday				
Tuesday				
Wednesday				
Thursday				
Friday				
Saturday				
Sunday				

WEEK 8

	Step, Level	Heart Rate	Other Exercises	Activities
Monday				
Tuesday				
Wednesday				
Thursday				
Friday				
Saturday				
Sunday				

MONTH 2 Progress Record

Waist: _____

Chest: _____

Weight: _____

Results of pinch test: _____

Results of poke test: _____

Number of sit-ups: _____

Changes in appearance: _____

How I feel: _____

_____

_____

_____

WEEK 9

	Step, Level	Heart Rate	Other Exercises	Activities
Monday				
Tuesday				
Wednesday				
Thursday				
Friday				
Saturday				
Sunday				

WEEK 10

	Step, Level	Heart Rate	Other Exercises	Activities
Monday				
Tuesday				
Wednesday				
Thursday				
Friday				
Saturday				
Sunday				

WEEK 11

	Step, Level	Heart Rate	Other Exercises	Activities
Monday				
Tuesday				
Wednesday				
Thursday				
Friday				
Saturday				
Sunday				

WEEK 12

	Step, Level	Heart Rate	Other Exercises	Activities
Monday				
Tuesday				
Wednesday				
Thursday				
Friday				
Saturday				
Sunday				

MONTH 3 Progress Record

Waist: _____

Chest: _____

Weight: _____

Results of pinch test: _____

Results of poke test: _____

Number of sit-ups: _____

Changes in appearance: _____

How I feel: _____

_____

_____

_____

_____

WEEK 13

	Step, Level	Heart Rate	Other Exercises	Activities
Monday				
Tuesday				
Wednesday				
Thursday				
Friday				
Saturday				
Sunday				

WEEK 14

	Step, Level	Heart Rate	Other Exercises	Activities
Monday				
Tuesday				
Wednesday				
Thursday				
Friday				
Saturday				
Sunday				

WEEK 15

	Step, Level	Heart Rate	Other Exercises	Activities
Monday				
Tuesday				
Wednesday				
Thursday				
Friday				
Saturday				
Sunday				

WEEK 16

	Step, Level	Heart Rate	Other Exercises	Activities
Monday				
Tuesday				
Wednesday				
Thursday				
Friday				
Saturday				
Sunday				

MONTH 4 Progress Record

Waist: _____

Chest: _____

Weight: _____

Results of pinch test: _____

Results of poke test: _____

Number of sit-ups: _____

Changes in appearance: _____

How I feel: _____

_____

_____

_____

_____

WEEK 17

	Step, Level	Heart Rate	Other Exercises	Activities
Monday				
Tuesday				
Wednesday				
Thursday				
Friday				
Saturday				
Sunday				

WEEK 18

	Step, Level	Heart Rate	Other Exercises	Activities
Monday				
Tuesday				
Wednesday				
Thursday				
Friday				
Saturday				
Sunday				

WEEK 19

	Step, Level	Heart Rate	Other Exercises	Activities
Monday				
Tuesday				
Wednesday				
Thursday				
Friday				
Saturday				
Sunday				

WEEK 20

	Step, Level	Heart Rate	Other Exercises	Activities
Monday				
Tuesday				
Wednesday				
Thursday				
Friday				
Saturday				
Sunday				

MONTH 5 Progress Record

Waist: _____

Chest: _____

Weight: _____

Results of pinch test: _____

Results of poke test: _____

Number of sit-ups: _____

Changes in appearance: _____

How I feel: _____

_____

_____

_____

213

Counting
Calories

There is only one way to keep weight off: you must turn the food you eat into energy rather than store it as fat. The following chart will give you an idea of the number of calories used for energy during some of the most common recreational and home-maintenance activities.

CALORIES USED PER HOUR

Activity	Body Weight:	100 Pounds	150 Pounds	200 Pounds
Archery		245	295	345
Badminton				
singles recreational		275	330	385
doubles recreational		235	285	335
Baseball				
pitcher only		305	370	435
catcher only		270	330	385
other players		220	265	310
Basketball				
game (full court, continuous)		585	710	830
nongame, ½ court, etc.		435	525	615
officiating		435	525	615
Bench stepping—30 steps				
per minute				
7"		480	575	675
12"		625	755	885
16"		870	1050	1230
18"		1095	1325	1550
Bicycling				
5½ mph		190	230	270
10 mph		325	395	460
13 mph		515	620	725

Activity	Body Weight:	100 Pounds	150 Pounds	200 Pounds
Bowling				
continuous		210	255	300
regular		150	180	610
Calisthenics (general)		235	285	335
Canoeing				
2 mph		235	285	335
4 mph		490	595	695
Chopping wood				
automatically (power saw)		175	210	245
hand		355	425	500
Dancing				
fox trot		195	240	280
contemporary (rock, disco)		195	240	280
polka		425	510	600
rumba		235	285	335
square		330	400	465
waltz		195	240	280
Digging		390	475	555
Fencing				
recreational		235	285	335
competitive (vigorous)		480	575	675

CALORIES USED PER HOUR

Activity	Body Weight:	100 Pounds	150 Pounds	200 Pounds
CALORIES USED PER HOUR				
Fishing				
boat		105	125	150
ice		140	170	195
stream (wading)		235	285	335
standing (little movement)		120	145	170
surf		140	170	195
Football				
playground (touch)		470	565	665
tackle		660	795	930
officiating		435	525	615
Gardening (weeding, hoeing, digging, and spading)		305	365	430
Golf				
twosome 9 holes in 1½ hours (carrying clubs)		295	360	420
twosome 9 holes in 1½ hours (pull clubs)		260	315	370
foursome 9 holes in 2 hours (carry clubs)		210	255	295
foursome 9 holes in 2 hours (pull clubs)		195	240	280

Activity	Body Weight: 100 Pounds	150 Pounds	200 Pounds
Gymnastics			
light	235	285	335
medium	400	485	565
hard	555	670	785
Handball			
2 people	610	735	860
cut throat	470	565	665
4 people	400	485	565
Hiking			
20-lb. pack, 2 mph	235	285	335
20-lb. pack, 3½ mph	300	360	420
20-lb. pack, 4 mph	355	425	500
Hill climbing	470	565	665
Hockey			
ice	705	850	1000
field	705	850	1000
Horseback riding			
trot	325	395	460
walk	130	155	185
gallop	470	565	665
Horseshoes	180	220	255
Jogging (5.5 mph)	515	620	725

CALORIES USED PER HOUR

Activity	Body Weight:	100 Pounds	150 Pounds	200 Pounds
Judo		620	750	875
Karate		620	750	875
Lawn mowing				
push		360	435	510
power (must push)		210	255	300
power		195	240	280
sitting		115	135	160
Lacrosse		705	850	1000
Mountain climbing		470	565	665
Orienteering		470	565	665
Painting house		165	195	230
Paperhanging		165	195	230
Pick & shovel work (continuous)		315	380	445
Pool		120	145	170
Raking leaves and dirt		175	210	245
Ropeskipping				
50-60 skips left foot only (per min.)		400	485	565
70-80 skips left foot only (per min.)		435	525	615
90-100 skips left foot only (per min.)		515	620	725

CALORIES USED PER HOUR

Activity	Body Weight:	100 Pounds	150 Pounds	200 Pounds
110-120 skips left foot only (per min.)		705	850	1000
130-140 skips left foot only (per min.)		940	1135	1330
Rowing				
pleasure—2 mph		235	285	335
vigorous—4 mph		515	620	725
Rowing machine				
easy		235	285	335
vigorous		515	620	725
Run in place				
50-60 steps per min. (left foot only)		400	485	565
70-80 steps per min. (left foot only)		435	525	615
90-100 steps per min. (left foot only)		515	620	725
110-120 steps per min. (left foot only)		705	850	1000
130-140 steps per min. (left foot only)		940	1135	1330

CALORIES USED PER HOUR

Activity	Body Weight: 100 Pounds	150 Pounds	200 Pounds
Running			
5.5 mph	515	620	725
7.2 mph	550	660	775
8 mph	625	755	885
8.7 mph	705	850	1000
11.4 mph	955	1155	1355
12.5 mph	1120	1470	1720
Sprinting	1915	2310	2705
Sanding floors (power)	180	220	255
Sailing			
calm water	120	145	170
rough water	145	175	205
Sawing			
hand	305	370	435
power	180	220	255
Scuba diving	355	425	500
Shooting			
pistol	125	150	180
rifle	145	175	205
Skating (leisure)			
ice	275	330	385
roller	275	330	385

	CALORIES USED PER HOUR			
Activity	Body Weight:	100 Pounds	150 Pounds	200 Pounds
Skating (vigorous)				
ice		485	590	690
roller		485	590	690
Skiing				
downhill (continuous riding and lifts not included)		465	560	660
cross country—5 mph		550	660	775
cross country—9 mph		785	945	1105
Skin diving		355	425	500
Sledding		335	405	470
Snowshoeing 2.2 mph		300	360	420
Snowshoveling				
light		475	575	675
heavy		825	995	1170
Snowmobiling		160	195	225
Soccer		470	565	665
Stationary bicycle: resistance sufficient to get pulse rate to 130				
10 mph		330	400	465
15 mph		515	620	725
20 mph		700	840	985

Activity	Body Weight:	100 Pounds	150 Pounds	200 Pounds
			CALORIES USED PER HOUR	
Swimming (crawl)				
20 yards per minute		235	285	335
30 yards per minute		330	400	465
35 yards per minute		425	510	600
40 yards per minute		470	565	665
45 yards per minute		540	650	765
55 yards per minute		660	795	930
Table tennis				
recreational		235	285	335
vigorous		355	425	500
Tennis (singles)				
recreational		335	405	470
competitive		470	565	665
Tennis (doubles)				
recreational		235	285	335
competitive		335	405	470
Treadmill				
3 mph		235	285	335
4 mph		270	330	385
5.5 mph		515	620	725
7.2 mph		625	755	885
8 mph		705	850	1000

CALORIES USED PER HOUR

Activity	Body Weight:	100 Pounds	150 Pounds	200 Pounds
Volleyball				
recreational		275	330	385
competitive		470	565	665
Walking				
2 mph		145	175	205
2½ mph		200	240	285
3 mph		235	285	335
3½ mph		245	300	350
4 mph		270	330	385
4½ mph		355	425	500
5 mph		435	525	615
5½ mph		515	620	725
upstairs (normal)		355	425	500
upstairs, 2 at a time (rapidly)		785	945	1105
downstairs (normal)		355	425	500
Water skiing		375	455	535
Weight training (does not include super sets)		235	285	335
Weeding		235	285	335
Window cleaning		180	220	255
Wrestling		620	750	875
Yoga		180	220	255